HOW TO TALK ABOUT LEGACY GIVING

YOUR GUIDE TO CREATING INSPIRING LEGACY MESSAGES

Aimée Lindenberger, CFRE

How to Talk About Legacy Giving:
Your guide to creating inspiring legacy messages
Copyright © 2024 Aimée Lindenberger

Library and Archives Canada Cataloguing in Publication

Title: How to talk about legacy giving: your guide to creating inspiring legacy messages / by Aimée Lindenberger.
Names: Lindenberger, Aimée, author.
Description: Series statement: Legacy giving essentials; book one | Includes bibliographical references.
Identifiers: Canadiana (print) 20240328108 | Canadiana (ebook) 20240328124 | ISBN 9781998796113 (softcover) | ISBN 9781998796120 (EPUB)
Subjects: LCSH: Fund raising — Canada. | LCSH: Nonprofit organizations — Canada — Finance. | LCSH: Legacies — Canada.
Classification: LCC HV41.9.C3 L56 2024 | DDC 361.7068/1 — dc23

Publisher: Civil Sector Press

Box 86, Station C, Toronto, Ontario, M6J 3M7 Canada
Telephone: 416.267.1287
www.charityinfo.ca | www.hilborn-civilsectorpress.com

Editor: **Marlena McCarthy**
Book design: **John VanDuzer, wishart.net**

We acknowledge that the land where we live and work is the traditional territory of many nations from across Turtle Island, and is covered by the Dish With One Spoon Wampum Belt Covenant, an agreement between the Haudenosaunee and the Ojibway and allied nations, including the Mississaugas, the Anishnaabeg, the Chippewa, and the Wendat peoples to peaceably share and care for the lands around the Great Lakes of North America. This land today is home to many diverse First Nations, Inuit, and Métis peoples. We honour and thank them for their stewardship of these lands, and stand committed to be partners in truth-seeking, healing, reconciliation, and justice for all.

HOW TO TALK ABOUT LEGACY GIVING
YOUR GUIDE TO CREATING INSPIRING LEGACY MESSAGES

Aimée Lindenberger, CFRE

LEGACY GIVING · ESSENTIALS · 1

TABLE OF CONTENTS

vii

FOREWORD

Legacy giving is about weaving the generosity of individuals into the fabric of our future. It's about creating enduring impacts that resonate beyond lifetimes. And it's by far the most cost-effective way to raise money for charities and support their work to make our world a better place.

Yet, despite the importance of legacy giving for supporters and the significant impact it has on the causes they love, there has been a noticeable gap in practical and insightful literature on the subject. Well, not anymore!

How to Talk about Legacy Giving is a much-needed resource in a field where nuanced communication is key. Having held senior roles in major and legacy gift fundraising, I have been one of many eagerly encouraging Aimée Lindenberger to put pen to paper. In this book, Aimée shares with us her deep understanding of the art of legacy giving communications. She helps us to effectively talk to supporters about legacy giving — whether in person or on paper.

And this book is just the beginning. It lays the groundwork for an informative five-part series, where each subsequent book delves deeper into the legacy engagement process. Take the next book, *How to Engage Potential Legacy Donors: Your Guide to Initial Outreach and Connection*. It's a crucial next step in the journey. It dives deep into proactive strategies for reaching potential legacy donors, something I know through experience to be absolutely vital.

As you turn these pages, know that you're tapping into a wealth of knowledge and experience. This book, and the ones to come, are more than guides; they are catalysts for change in the way we approach legacy giving.

I'm so pleased to introduce this series, knowing without a doubt that it will help ensure our collective future is shaped by generosity and vision.

Jane Westheuser, CFRE
Associate, Refocus Fundraising

Former Senior Manager, Legacy Giving,
Heart & Stroke Canada

Former Major Gift Officer, Faculty of Law and Faculty of Medicine, University of British Columbia

Author of the Legacy Giving chapter of Excellence in Fundraising in Canada, Volume One, *2nd edition*

PREFACE

We don't have to make it so hard.

We've made talking about legacy giving so complicated for so long, but we truly don't have to.

Legacy giving, really, is about what people care about most, and what they want the future to look like. That's all.

This book will help you see how easy it can be to talk to people about legacy giving — in person, in writing, and in your organization's communications — and then give you some tangible tools and things to try to create legacy messaging that works for you.

By the end, I hope you'll feel empowered. Empowered and able to communicate your legacy message simply and easily. Free of worry that you can get it wrong, or that it is terribly complex and stressful.

Because it doesn't have to be.

Legacy giving, really, is about what people care about most, and what they want the future to look like. That's all.

HOW TO TALK ABOUT LEGACY GIVING

WHY HAVE WE MADE IT SO HARD TO TALK ABOUT LEGACY GIVING?

———————————

Let's face it.

For many people, legacy giving — also known as "planned giving", "gift planning", "gift and estate planning" among other names — is inherently tied to something most people don't want to talk about.

Death.

In fact, you may be reading this now thinking — "Ugh, do I

really want to think about death right now?" or, "Maybe I'll read this later…"

Well, you'll be happy to know this means you are a properly functioning human being!

You see, the human mind has a host of unconscious "death-reminder avoidance" behaviours that we are very rarely aware of even when we are engaging in them ourselves.

They're likely trying to work their sneaky avoidance magic on you right now — but stick with me as it will be worth it, I swear!

There are some big concepts behind all of this, but we're going to follow "Aimée's First Rule of Writing for Humans™" in this book, so, for now, we'll keep it simple. But if you're a word nerd, data nerd, research-reading fiend, or a delightful combination of them all, like me, check out the references at the end of the book for more.

Aimée's First Rule of Writing for Humans™

• • •

When writing for humans, write like a human.

I promise, we're not going to delve into death all that much, but I think we need to spend a little bit of time on why we don't want to talk about it, so we can overcome these obstacles and make it easier to talk about legacy giving.

How we think about — and avoid thinking about — death

What are your first thoughts when you see the word *death?*

For many, it can conjure thoughts of fear, loss, the unknown, grief, pain, illness, losing loved ones or leaving those you care about behind. The word death gets you thinking about your own mortality.

Researchers of all kinds — psychologists, sociologists, neurologists, linguists and more — study all manner of things related to how we think about death.

- What words come to mind?
- What emotions does it evoke?
- Which areas of the brain are involved?
- What diversion strategies does the mind employ to avoid the topic?

And this is just the tip of the thanatological research iceberg!

Thanatology

•••

Per Merriam Webster: the description or study of the phenomena of death and of psychological mechanisms for coping with them.

While we'll only scratch the surface here, these areas play a huge role in crafting compelling and effective legacy giving messaging.

In research, when people are asked which words describe their feelings about death, the most commonly mentioned are inevitable, *fear, sad, final, scary, los*s — and for some, *peace* and *natural* too.[1]

Emotionally? Death is scary! It causes anxiety for many people and in some cases even outright phobias, but even those who are not actively afraid often view the topic of death as uncomfortable, taboo, or highly private. People can feel irritated, disrespected, or violated by a conversation they believe is getting uncomfortably close to their personal mortality.

The mere word itself — death — has an emotional weight and gravity far more than its five letters can account for. You may have felt this for yourself at the beginning of the book. Researchers measure this as *valence* (the degree of positive or negative connotation) and *arousal* (the degree of emotional intensity or calmness) and death has both a very negative valence and a high degree of arousal intensity. In short, death is a big, bad, scary word.

And so, people don't want to talk about death. People don't want to think about it. Donors don't want to hear about it. And fundraisers don't want to ask for gifts related to it.

You see the pickle we have here?

But wait!
It gets scarier!
———————

Well, not really — but I wanted to prepare you for what I'm about to introduce next, which sounds rather scary, and that is an area of social and evolutionary psychology known as Terror Management Theory (TMT).

I can almost hear the ominous organ music now!

In all seriousness though, TMT is an incredibly powerful way to understand what we as humans contend with every day as mortal beings. In their book, *The Worm at the Core:*

On the Role of Death in Life[2] authors Sheldon Solomon, Jeff Greenberg and Tom Pyszczynski note:

> *"The awareness that we humans will die*
> *has a profound and pervasive effect on*
> *our thoughts, feelings, and behaviors in almost every*
> *domain of human life —*
> *whether we are conscious of it or not."*

Their work builds on that of Ernest Becker and his Pulitzer Prize-winning book *The Denial of Death*. The basic tenets of this area of study say:

1. Human beings live our lives with the knowledge that one day we will die.
2. Knowing we will die is rather crippling if we are actively aware of this every day — so we generally avoid anything that makes us contemplate this fact.
3. One of the main ways to soothe the terror we feel about dying is through a belief that it is possible to transcend death in some way.

There is more to it than that of course — but this book is about legacy giving messaging, so we'll stop there, as this already has two major implications for our purposes. First, we avoid reminders of our own death whenever possible; and second, we humans look for ways we can transcend death in some way, such as through a belief in the afterlife or reincarnation, taking comfort in the idea that our bloodline continues through our descendants, or doing things to ensure that we will live on in the memories of others.

Let's start with the first of these two relevant issues — that we generally avoid reminders of our own mortality.

Death-Reminder Avoidance

I first came across the area of Terror Management Theory in 2013, through the work of Dr. Russell James.

In his book, *Inside the Mind of the Bequest Donor* [3] he summed up the death-reminder avoidance strategies as the 5 Ds:

DISTRACT — Focusing on something else to avoid the topic — "I have something else I need to do."

DIFFERENTIATE — Seeking ways the situation is different — "I'm not like them. I'm going to live a long time because I don't drive too fast/eat fried food..."

DENY — Believing data to be false or overstated — "Sure, maybe smoking causes cancer, but I know lots of people who smoke and none of us have cancer. It can't be as bad as they say."

DELAY — Putting off thinking about it for later — "Yes, this is important and I will deal with it at some point, but not right now."

DEPART — Leaving the reminder behind — "I am not going to think about this!"

Some of these probably seem familiar to you if you've worked in legacy giving — or, if you've ever tried to have a conversation with a loved one about getting their estate plans in order — or, if you've ever tried to motivate yourself to get your own Will written or updated!

Our brains are like disgruntled teens avoiding chores when

it comes to having to think about anything related to death. They'll try to distract themselves. They'll find other things to think about if they can. They'll find reasons they shouldn't have to. They'll tell themselves they'll do it later but just keep putting it off. They just don't wanna.

It's why a surprising number of lawyers,[4] advisors and those in the legacy giving field find ourselves procrastinating about writing or updating our Wills. We know better — but we still put it off!

It's because *we're human.*

But, with all those death-reminder avoidance behaviours at play not only among the supporters we wish to engage about legacy giving, but also among the very human fundraisers and decision-makers at charities as well, what has the general strategy of a lot of planned giving messaging looked like?

Logical. Prudent.
Financial. Decisions.

Given that our starting position is one where generally fund-raisers and charities didn't want to talk about death, and their supporters didn't want to hear about or think about death — it makes all kinds of sense that the instinct has been to sidestep any scary feelings and make the conversation an intellectual one. That way, planned giving messaging could be about very logical, prudent (but complex!) financial decisions and shift these conversations to a so-called "left-side-of-the-brain" choice, as devoid of emotion as it could be.

And so, planned giving became the realm of experts —

financial experts, estate planning experts, life insurance experts, tax experts and legal experts. Charities with planned giving programs tried to be a bridge between their cause and all of these areas, acting as lay advisors.

Aimée, don't you think we need advisors?
• • •
We definitely need advisors! And lawyers, trust officers, insurance brokers, accountants, estate planners, and all the other vital people in the grand collage we build together in this sector.

I count many as friends and colleagues — and I rely on them for their expertise. But I don't try to do their jobs for them, and they definitely don't attempt to do mine.

Remember that allied professionals are there to help — they very much want to help! So let them do what they're best at, and you can focus on what you're best at — building relationships with supporters and raising funds to do good work in the world.

Fundraisers who specialized in planned giving often "worked their way up to it" after years or even decades in other fund development areas. Many spent hundreds, or sometimes thousands, of dollars on special training courses to learn highly technical information about a wide variety of gift planning vehicles.

And with this newfound knowledge, donor information packages were created.

Two-page information sheets! Presentation folders with arrays of info sheets outlining every gift type! Downloadable resources on websites! Multi-page booklets of information!! Gift illustration charts!!!

You may be saying — how could this be bad? As a self-confessed data-nerd, reader, and lover of communicating with donors surely, Aimée, you would love that charities created all these pieces to share information with their supporters about their options — plus, look at all those exclamation points!

Well, there are a few problems with this approach.

1. The "Jam Paradox";
2. For most charities, complex gift types are received very rarely; and
3. Legacy giving decisions aren't based on information or logic.

The 'Jam Paradox'

If you've ever come to one of my sessions at a conference, or heck, if you've ever talked to me about legacy giving marketing just casually over coffee, you've probably heard me talk about the jam paradox.*

To me, it is vitally important to understand this concept as we look at where we're at as a sector with legacy giving marketing and its successes and failures in gaining legacy gifts for charitable organizations.

---

* Why do I call it the "jam paradox" instead of the "paradox of choice"? While it is known by both names, the "jam paradox" captures people's attention and they wonder — "How could jam be paradoxical?" It is a way to surprise and delight an audience — giving them an emotional impact that the "paradox of choice" doesn't provide. And when they hear the story, the concept is much more likely to "stick" with them! Using language that can surprise and delight is a prime way to help your legacy messaging stick, too!

The jam paradox, or "paradox of choice" takes its name from a series of experiments where researchers set up a display of jams for shoppers to sample. Participants could try as many as they liked, and they would receive a $1 coupon toward the purchase of a jar of jam.

On one day, **24** different jams were available to try.

On another day, **6** different jams were available to try.

And what did researchers find?

People were *ten times more likely* to buy jam when there were *fewer* options to choose from.

Why is this? Well, too many choices can cause decision paralysis.

When presented with more options, people often struggle to decide which one is the *best* option.

They don't want to make a mistake or pick something that they might be less satisfied with later — so they often defer a choice thinking they'll decide later, or sometimes, they decide to choose nothing at all!

Now, if a relatively simple decision like which jam to buy is hampered this much by increasing the number of options, how much more difficult are we making legacy giving — something that is a much more high-stakes, high-dollar-value decision that has great personal meaning for people — when we add additional complexity to the mix?

I'd bet you a jar of strawberry-rhubarb jam it's a lot!

But I don't have to bet. Studies[6] have found that the more complex the decision, the more important it is to keep choice options limited. And similarly, when it is difficult to compare alternatives, and when people want to make a decision quickly — you want to keep the number of choice points limited. And, I'd argue that even though a legacy giving decision often takes 2–3 years to go from interest to acting on the decision, people don't want to spend a lot of time actively thinking about the options given the death-reminder avoidance issues we discussed.

So, knowing that legacy giving is a complex, sensitive decision that is adjacent to a topic people generally don't like to think about — we need to do everything we can to simplify our message and avoid triggering decision paralysis with too many options.

Receiving complex gift types is rare for most charities

For the past few decades, charities have sent donors information packages outlining virtually every legacy gift option, and many list multiple gift vehicles with equal prominence on their websites.

Perhaps it wouldn't be so bad if people were choosing these options. But, for most charities, receiving complex gift types is incredibly rare. And as we just learned above, having too many options can hamper a donor's ability to decide to create a legacy gift.

Mercifully, most organizations are no longer actively show-casing Charitable Gift Annuities or Charitable Remainder Trusts. But alongside the most common gift type — gifts in Wills (a.k.a. Bequests) — donors often have to wade through information on gifts of life insurance; gifts of RRSPs, RRIFs, or TSFAs; gifts of securities; gifts of real estate or other property, and more. Even just seeing that list of legacy gift types would make some people break out in hives. Imagine trying to read about each one and decide which is right for you if you know nothing about most of them?*

Confessions of a printing industry alum

. . .

In my previous life in the printing industry, we used to print these snazzy staggered information sheet sets on glossy paper by the boxload. At the time I didn't wonder overly much what happened to them. But now I know the unfortunate truth.

Most of these legacy giving information packages sit on a shelf, or in a filing cabinet, or in a box shoved under someone's desk until they need to get recycled because the tax information or regulations changed.

The reality is, most donors aren't looking for information. And those that are, aren't looking for information about every gift type under the sun.

The simple fact is, for most charities, between 95-98% of the legacy gifts they receive are gifts in Wills.

---

* It makes sense if you think about it — 1/3 of the legacy gift vehicles are death reminders — "bequests", "life insurance"; 1/3 are tax-related (another highly negative association) — "RRSPs", "RRIFs", and "TSFAs"; and 1/3 are financial products out of reach for many — "securities", "real estate".

Even organizations who have been actively marketing other types of gifts for years find their donors overwhelmingly choose the most straightforward legacy gift — a gift in their Will.

This is why I encourage organizations — whether they're small, medium-sized, or some of the biggest in the country — to keep their legacy marketing messages focussed on the simple option that everyone loves: *gifts in Wills.*

In my experience, donors who are interested in other gift types most often have their own financial planner who is advising them on a particular strategy. They are not looking to be educated by the charity, *they just need to know the legacy gift option they're considering is possible for your charity to work with.*

Legacy giving decisions are not based on information or logic

So far, we've discussed two major pitfalls with presenting a variety of gift types and making legacy giving about a "prudent financial decision":

1) The jam paradox can cause decision paralysis, potentially leading many to procrastinate about making a decision, or deciding to make no choice at all! Legacy decisions are high stakes, high dollar value, deeply personal and meaningful decisions. They are genuinely big decisions. So, it is even more important to simplify choices to avoid overwhelming people.

2) The vast majority of legacy donors still choose gifts

in Wills despite charities actively marketing other gift types for years. Featuring these seldom used legacy gift types is adding complexity for donors to wade through and complications for fundraisers without any significant benefit.

But there is one other big issue, which, I believe, is the root of all the above issues. And it's where the second major implication of Terror Management Theory in legacy giving comes into play.

Legacy giving decisions are not based on information or logic.

Legacy giving decisions are not made in the information processing part of our brains. They are not about information. They are not about logic.* Or prudence. Or planning.

Legacy giving decisions are made in the autobiographical part of the brain.

They are about who we are. Our life story. The thread it has woven, and how we imagine it continuing.

A legacy gift, really, is a person finding a way to ensure that what they find most important, most meaningful in this world, continues beyond themselves.

---

* To be fair, there are a small number of donors who do see a legacy gift primarily as a logical financial decision. They may be high-net worth donors who are creating legacy gifts for tax purposes and almost certainly have an advisor who has talked to them about the best option to achieve their financial goals. You don't need to convince them on the method, merely the vision — just like everyone else. So, when you tailor your messaging to the 99% rather than the 1%, you have the most appeal to all.

Sometimes, if we are lucky, we are part of an organization that has supporters who have been connected to the cause for 10 years, 20 years, 30 years — they've donated, they've volunteered, they've cared for decades! It is not just something they do; it is part of who they are. They share your organization's values; they imagine the same vision of a better future and want it to be realized even if they're not going to be there for it. And they trust you enough to see it through on their behalf.

That is legacy giving.

The logic of "Everyone should have a Will..."

• • •

Legacy marketing messaging using the logic-based argument, "Everyone should have a Will..." hasn't achieved big results over the years. People know they should have a Will and keep it updated. It is in our best interests, but just like the prudent financial decision approach, it is not activating the right part of the brain. Plus, no one likes to feel like a failure for not having done something they already know they should do.

All of this is well founded in research. It was Dr. Russell James' work with fMRI studies that showed that legacy giving questions "light up" the autobiographical parts of the brain. Dr. Jen Shang from the Institute of Sustainable Philanthropy in the UK has reams of findings on the importance of appealing to a donor's core values and how they see themself in giving decisions of all kinds.

And if we circle back to Terror Management Theory, legacy giving helps us see the thread of our life story continuing, which is a powerful way to soothe our very human terror about death — by transcending it in some way.

We will talk more about all of this in Chapter Two.

Let's be sure to ask the big question: If decades of legacy marketing centred on gift vehicles has resulted in less than 5% of donors creating legacy gifts, and knowing that the vast majority choose the simplest option (a gift in a Will) anyway — why are we still using this strategy? How could we do it differently?

"If you always do what you've always
done, you always get what you've always gotten."
— Jessie Potter, Director,
National Institute for Human Relationships

ENGAGE AND APPLY

1. How do you think your own attitudes about the topic of death affect your interest in legacy giving in your work life? How do they impact you as a donor?

2. How do people in your organization generally feel about legacy giving? Is it well understood and valued, or seen as daunting or off-putting in some way? If there are negative views of it, do you have a sense of what people find uncomfortable about legacy giving?

HOW CAN WE TALK
ABOUT LEGACY GIVING IN
A DIFFERENT WAY?

The good news is, talking about legacy giving is so much easier than we've been making it!

So, let's take a deep breath and let go of any preconceived notions that we need to be well-versed in tax planning, estate law, or financial vehicles to talk about legacy giving.

Let's start fresh.

Legacy giving — more than any other kind of giving — is about the person doing it.

It says something about who they are, what they believe, their values, the things they find meaningful, *and what they want the future to look like even though they won't be there to see it.* All these things come from within.

And, since the people creating legacy gifts already have all this within themselves, we don't really need to tell them anything, right? We don't need to inform, educate, or teach donors about legacy giving.

You don't need to be an expert to excite someone about the potential power of their legacy. You can simply talk to them about what they care about and the vision of a better future that you — and they — are trying to achieve.

Legacy giving is for everyone

• • •

When you take the stress out of talking about legacy giving, it opens it up for everyone:

Organizations that thought they didn't have the capacity to engage in legacy giving.

Board members who didn't want to tackle legacy giving for fear of getting it wrong.

Fundraisers who didn't consider legacy giving as a career option because it seemed elusive and complex.

Other departments who rebuffed integrating legacy messaging because they felt it seemed heavy and they feared it might depress other donations.

Donors who thought legacy gifts were only for the wealthy or financially savvy.

>ok at it with new eyes — because at
iι   'ust about what people care about
an   r future — and anyone can talk
abo

In the ..ainder of this chapter, we'll look at some of the foundational research behind this simpler approach to talking about legacy giving.

Legacy giving is about our life story

Occasionally charities receive "out-of-the-blue" legacy gifts from someone who had no prior giving history with them. But that is not the norm. Most often, legacy gifts come from donors who have long-time, sometimes many decades long, connections to your organization or cause.

These connections can be incredibly deep and multi-faceted. And while we may not always know what they are, they are virtually always there.

The specific connections may be things like a supporter's first motivation to get involved, or the circumstances going on in their life at the time, whether they've had friends or family connected to the cause, or perhaps they — or some-one they knew — directly benefitted from the work of the organization.

You may see signs of their deepening connection to your organization over time. Maybe they start volunteering in addition to giving, or they move from an annual donation to monthly giving, or they chip in for a capital campaign in addition to their regular gifts.* And sometimes the deepening of the connection is due to the sheer longevity of the attachment and the relationships built with those at the organization — the stories you've shared, the demonstrations of the impact their gifts have had, and a sense of progress on the big picture that has been achieved during those years. In all these things, you can see evidence of how your organization is woven throughout the supporter's life story.

These long-term autobiographical threads can show up in donor conversations or in legacy survey responses as statements like:

- "My first gift was when I was probably 13 years old. Our grade 8 class learned about polar bears, so I gave to protect them and the Arctic."
- "My grandfather always said your organization helped so much during the war."
- "ABC Hospital saved my son's life after he was in an accident."
- "Wow, I hadn't realized I've been a monthly donor for nearly 20 years!"
- "We had three generations out for the bird count today — it's become a family affair! Thank you for making sure there are birds in this world for our grandkids."

---

* A quick note to say that longevity of giving is more important than an ability to give larger gifts when it comes to legacy gift affinity. A donor who consistently gives $25 a year for 10 years or more would be much higher on my legacy prospect list than a donor who has given for three years plus contributed to a capital campaign. Personally, I believe we should be asking every donor to consider a legacy gift. When we need to prioritize our efforts due to time and/or budget constraints however, longevity of giving should be our guide.

- "Thank you for sharing the latest research update — I hope that soon no other mother will lose a child to X!"

Why are these connections so important?

Well, as Dr. Russell James found in a series of fMRI studies — where individuals were asked several questions about volunteering and giving to charity while in an MRI machine — asking people to contemplate legacy giving questions activates two parts of the brain:

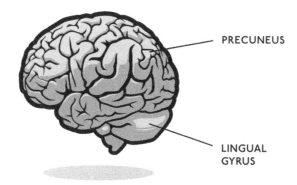

PRECUNEUS

LINGUAL GYRUS

1. The precuneus: sometimes called "the mind's eye", it is associated with visual imagery of memories and taking a view of oneself in the third person; and,
2. The lingual gyrus: an area also associated with the visual system, internal visualization, and dreaming.

Together, these two areas are thought to create what Dr. James has described as a sort of "visualized autobiography" or "visualization + 3rd person perspective on the self".

Let's say this in even simpler terms.

When people are considering legacy giving:

- their brain looks at their life story in a reflective way — as if from an outside perspective, and
- the areas involved are associated with memory and visualization.

The hypothesis is that for a supporter, the act of considering a legacy gift to a charity is about seeing the arc of how the gift fits within the story of their life up to now, and imagining their legacy as the continuation of their life story into the future.

The key with Dr. James' fMRI studies is that when the participants were considering the questions about volunteering or making an immediate gift, these areas of the brain were not activated in the same way.

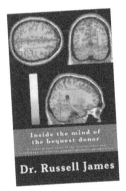

For brain science lovers

• • •

If you want to learn more, I highly recommend reading **Inside the Mind of the Bequest Donor** *to more deeply understand the studies Dr. Russell James conducted, as well as the science behind the areas of the brain that are activated when considering legacy giving. The book provides much more nuance on how his fMRI studies worked, and how the questions posed during the procedure were asked and interpreted. For those who want the full detail rather than my light overview – this is where you'll find it!*

Legacy giving messaging is much more successful when we understand and integrate these insights. By highlighting for donors the longevity of their involvement, the number of ways they have been connected over the years, and painting a picture of a better future that they can vividly imagine so they can see how their legacy can help bring it about, you will create legacy messaging that activates the right parts of a supporter's brain — a crucial step toward inspiring them to create a legacy gift.

Legacy giving is about who we are and what we're a part of

Just as the connections donors have with your organization play a big role in how they see you fitting into their life story, these connections also play a huge role in how donors see themselves.

Understanding how donors see themselves — and the various layers of identity involved — is tremendously useful in crafting legacy messaging.

This is where Philanthropic Psychology comes in.

Philanthropic Psychology

• • •

Philanthropic Psychology is an area of study pioneered by Dr. Jen Shang, and I had the pleasure of being one of the first in the world to complete her course at the Institute of Sustainable Philanthropy and receive a certification with distinction in Philanthropic Psychology. It is an incredibly important and growing field, and I highly encourage anyone involved in creating fundraising material to take this course if you can, as we will not even scratch the surface here.

When you think about who you are as a person — what comes to mind?

- Many people will start by listing their relationships to others — a mother, a sister, a friend.
- Others start with their area of work or profession — a fundraiser, an artist, a lawyer.
- Some will list personal characteristics — like smart, funny, or kind.
- Still others will talk about their national, regional, or community connections — a Canadian, a Newfoundlander, a Torontonian.

These are only a few components of our identities that inform how we see ourselves — and just a taste of those covered in Philanthropic Psychology.

In legacy giving, these identities and more(!) are useful to understand and integrate into your messaging. There are two especially important layers of identity I want to explore here:

- Organizational identity, and,
- Moral identity (part of personal identity)

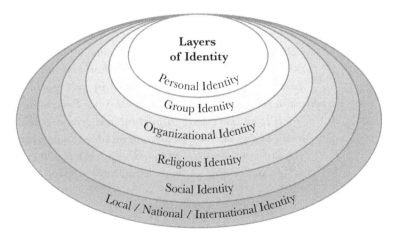

An **ORGANIZATIONAL IDENTITY** describes a person's identity in the context of their relationship to an organization. You may describe yourself as an employee of the organization you work for, or a member of a professional association, or the most important for our purposes here — a supporter of a particular charity.

When a person's connection to your organization is strong enough, they think of themselves as "a [charity name] donor" — for instance, a Heart & Stroke donor, or an Amnesty International supporter. Their attachment to your organization is part of who they are — part of who they believe themselves to be.

The people most likely to consider a legacy gift are those with a strong attachment to your organization — those who have integrated being a supporter of your organization into their identity.

Highlighting the various ways they are connected can reinforce and deepen this donor identity. You can help people realize the depths of their attachment by mentioning the different components of this identity — a donor, supporter, volunteer, ally, partner, or community member. Boost these identity attachments even further by reminding them how long this has been part of their identity — e.g., "a long-time supporter" or "a vital part of our community for over X years."

A **MORAL IDENTITY** describes the sort of person you see yourself as at your core. It is comprised of the deepest and most fundamental set of identity characteristics — for example, being kind, compassionate, caring, generous, trustworthy, loyal, or helpful.

Legacy donors are incredibly altruistic people. No one has to create a legacy gift for charity — but these people do. It is genuinely special, because it is still a small minority of people who choose to make a legacy gift. So — it's okay to highlight these things, it's not flattery, it's the truth!

A note about donor centricity

• • •

The concept of donor centricity — when taken to an inappropriate extreme — has undoubtedly led to donors being in a place of power over organizations or their communities in some cases. To me, this isn't donor centricity, it's "donor supremacy" — and nobody should be advocating for that.

But when we look at the original idea behind donor centricity — that we view donors as meaningful stakeholders of the organization and communicate the things that are important to them as a person rather than what we as an organization want to tell them — it is a valuable concept.

Sharing more about what is meaningful to people is good. Recognizing that people are acting in selfless ways for the benefit of others is okay.

Just make sure to keep it authentic.

When your messaging uses positive identity traits to reinforce how supporters see themselves, they feel closer to the organization, and get a feeling of well-being and alignment. They subconsciously (and occasionally consciously!), start to see that:

- This charity is a reflection of who I am
- This charity articulates many of my deepest thoughts and feelings
- My support of this charity reflects the core

of who I am
- This charity and I share many fundamental values and beliefs

Dr. Shang's research shows that when a strong donor identity and a group identity are both primed at the time people are making a donation decision, giving can increase up to 20%. So, you want to speak to them as a person, as an individual — with their own ideals, values, and beliefs — but also highlight that they are part of something bigger, united in a cause, joined with others working toward a better future.

This combination of speaking to the core of who your supporter believes themself to be and their alignment and attachment to your organization is highly successful when talking about legacy giving.

Legacy gifts are usually the largest and most personal gifts people ever make, and are a chance for donors to make a final statement about who they are and what they stand for.

Reinforce your supporter's sense of self in your legacy messaging — let them feel seen, understood, and valued as a person. Then talk about their connections to your organization — the longevity of the bond, the alignment in values — remind them that they are a part of a group that will be there, doing the work they believe in for years to come, and that their legacy can help make that possible.

And don't worry — you don't need to know all the ins-and-outs of Philanthropic Psychology — just remember that *legacy gifts are about who people are, and what they are part of,* and you'll be fine.

27

Legacy giving is about our vision of a better future (and a way to transcend death)

In addition to being about our life story, who we are, and what we're a part of, legacy gifts are about vision.

Not just your organization's vision. And not just the donor's vision.

The real magic of legacy giving is that it's about a shared vision of a better future you and your donor both want to achieve.

They've already been giving — *likely for years!* — helping to move closer to that better future. Even if your day-to-day communications are more caught up in the pressing needs of today or your latest campaign, your legacy giving message is the ideal time to talk about your big picture vision, and how you will move forward toward achieving it.

As mentioned before, Dr. James' research shows that when considering a legacy gift decision, one of the most active parts of the brain is the lingual gyrus — the part responsible for internal visualization and dreaming. So, help your supporters dream!

Help them see themselves having an impact in the future. Help them picture how years or decades from now, they are still making a difference for the cause they care about through their legacy.

It is both incredibly inspiring and comforting to people.

The inspirational element is pretty straightforward to understand. These people want to help. They care deeply about the cause, and their legacy is a chance to help more than they typically can during their lifetime. It's exciting!

But why comforting? Why do people get a sense of well-being and peace when they decide to make a legacy gift? It's because it addresses some of our most deep, underlying fears — we will die, we will no longer exist, we will be forgotten, and our lives will have been meaningless.

Hoo-boy! That's some existential angst right there.

So, the short answer to why creating a legacy gift is comforting is because it's one way to alleviate some of this angst and anxiety.

This brings us back to Terror Management Theory.

As a recap — TMT says three things that are very important for legacy giving:

1. We all live our lives knowing we will die.
2. It would be impossible to function if we were consciously aware of this fact all the time, so we have lots of ingrained behaviours that help us avoid thinking about our mortality.
3. We look to soothe our terror about our inevitable death through a belief that it is possible to transcend death in some way.

Ultimately, what quells this terror is a belief in some sort of literal or symbolic immortality.

In *The Worm at the Core: On the Role of Death in Life*, the authors say this on symbolic immortality:

"[One] means of achieving immortality is to assure that some aspect of one's identity, or some legacy of one's existence, will live on after death. This symbolic immortality promises that we will still be part of something eternal after our last breath, that some symbolic vestige of the self will persist in perpetuity."

The drive to have our lives matter and to not simply fade out of memory is at the heart of so many of our decisions, behaviours, and beliefs. Whether it is a belief in the afterlife, a sense that we live on through our children and grandchildren, or a desire to create a great work of art or scientific break-through that will ensure we will be remembered, we — *consciously or unconsciously* — look for opportunities to assure ourselves that some part of us is permanent.

Legacy gifts are one way people can feel they will still matter even after they're gone. They will still make an impact; they will still be present in some way for your work in the future.

It's reassuring. It gives people some relief from their existential anxiety.

Want to learn more about TMT but
don't love reading somewhat academic books?

• • •

While I highly recommend reading "The Worm at the Core:
On the Role of Death in Life" *and* "The Denial of Death" —
they're not exactly light reading! So if that's not your
cup of tea, you can get a great overview of TMT from this
recorded seminar delivered by Sheldon Solomon,
one of the authors of The Worm at the Core:
https://bit.ly/TerrorManagementTheory

Sometimes, people talk about the "peace of mind" they get from simply getting their Will written.

But a legacy gift provides them with a much deeper peace of mind — the peace of knowing that their life will be meaningful long past the time they die. Getting their Will finalized is usually a somewhat fleeting joy, yet the comfort people feel once they've decided to create a legacy gift can go on for years because it represents a symbolic immortality.

This symbolic immortality can be a touchstone donors return to in their minds again and again. Boost this well-being by making sure your legacy messaging is continuing to affirm for people that these gifts are meaningful, and that the people who make them are an important part of the work yet to come. Paint that picture of the better future and remind them that their legacy can help get one step closer to achieving it.

Good legacy messaging doesn't have to be complicated.

If you can talk to people about who they are and what they care about — you can talk about legacy giving.

If you can talk to people about what your vision of a better future is — you can talk about legacy giving.

Truly — that's essentially all you need to start engaging supporters in considering a legacy gift.

In Chapter Three, we'll look at some of the nuances of how legacy messaging is different from most organizational or fundraising messaging to help you build on these essentials and create powerful legacy communications.

ENGAGE AND APPLY

1. Reflect on your own life story and the connections you have with a charitable organization or cause. How have these connections influenced your giving and involvement over time?

2. Consider the different layers of your identity — personal, professional, community-related. How does being connected to a charitable organization align with who you see yourself as? How does this connection contribute to your sense of identity?

3. If a supporter's legacy is a way to continue the work they believe in, how might this translate to their sense of well-being? How would you subtly plant the seed in your messaging that creating a legacy gift can provide supporters with a sense of comfort about the meaning of their life?

4. How does talking about legacy giving with a focus on personal values, identity, and beliefs resonate with you? Do you feel it might make it easier for you to engage supporters in considering legacy giving? Why or why not?

LEGACY MESSAGING
IS VERY DIFFERENT FROM OTHER
NONPROFIT MESSAGING

So far, we've considered some of the big-picture issues at play in legacy messaging, namely:

- how it has been overcomplicated in the past and is perhaps actively hampering donors' decision-making,
- how we can instead align our legacy messaging with the reasons donors choose to be connected to our organizations over the long term, and,

- how we can share our vision for the future and the core aspects of what it means to be human — who we are, what we believe, and what we want the future to look like.

There is one other layer that stands in the way of widespread success with legacy messaging for organizations.

Legacy messaging is very different from other types of nonprofit messaging — and most organizations do not have the internal capacity to create it.

Now, this is not anyone's fault.

Legacy messaging is a struggle for most organizations because it is so niche, and because its nuances are not generally well understood.

Some nonprofits have communications teams that specialize in PR, media relations, or organizational communications, whereas others may have a writer who excels at annual appeals, grant writing, or other immediate revenue-generating fundraising. The very large and very lucky may be fortunate enough to have both, while smaller organizations most often do not have either.

Very few organizations have communications specialists in-house with a background in creating legacy messaging, however. So, when someone who is used to writing in a formal organizational voice tries to write very human-centred legacy messaging — or when an immediate fundraising expert is writing to urge donors to "create your legacy today!" — well, neither works very well at all for legacy giving.

Legacy messaging requires a completely different tone and intimacy level than organizational-level communications, and is much softer, less urgent, and has a much longer appeal cycle than general fundraising communications.

In-house fundraisers and communications team members are, of course, very smart, resourceful people however — so to figure out how to create this unique messaging type they do what any sensible person would think is the best option: they look at what other charities are doing with their legacy marketing, with the assumption, "Surely, it must be working for them!"

Sadly, this often creates a vicious cycle of producing yet more multi-page info sheets, Freedom 55-style brochures, and newsletters featuring articles explaining the different types of life insurance policies or stories about how easy someone found it to create their Will.

Dearest reader, it makes me want to cry.

Because these types of communications are not working. Unless, of course, you think that charities engaging fewer than 5% of their donors in legacy giving is success.

And yet, because legacy messaging is so niche… and because so many organizations have been using the same approach for so long… and because those looking for guidance don't know what they don't know, we end up with even more organizations thinking this is the way legacy messaging has to be done.

The result is this pervasive idea that 5% engagement in legacy giving is the best you can expect.

But, *what if... it could all be different?*

Change the way you look at things, and the things you look at change*
———

We can turn everything on its head if, rather than saying "What has been done in the past?" or "What is everyone else doing?", we approach things from a more curious place.

Ask yourself: *"What do we want the reader to think, feel, and do?"* I ask myself this question every time I sit down to write any fundraising communications piece — and it is particularly useful when writing legacy messaging.

It may sound a little tactical, but this approach helps us consider the reader — and their thoughts and feelings — and put those at the heart of what we create. It's a big shift from what many organizations do, which is focussing *on what the organization wants* to be telling people or what they think *they should be* telling them based on what they've seen done elsewhere.

Making this shift is so much more effective for nonprofits and more meaningful for donors. But when you are creating something new without the guardrails of the past to go by, you want to be doubly sure you understand the nuances of how legacy giving is different from other types of messaging so you can set yourself up for success.

———

* I'm not really a motivational speaker fan — but I do love this quote from Dr. Wayne Dyer. It concisely captures the shift in perspective I think we would do well to apply to legacy giving messaging.

So, let's look at some of the ways legacy giving messaging is unique — different from both organizational messaging and general fundraising messaging. This will help us later when we get to Chapter 6 and start putting it all together to create some legacy messaging.

How legacy giving messaging is different from broad organizational messaging

The messaging you see on an organization's website, in a press release, or in an annual report is quite different from legacy fundraising communications because it is very inward-focused — the organization talks a lot about themselves to establish who they are, what they do, and to demonstrate credibility.

Large organizations, particularly hospitals, health organizations, and universities face a greater challenge than most because they must demonstrate incredibly high degrees of expertise, an impeccably solid structure, and absolute professionalism.

This messaging requires a balancing act because it must speak to a wide variety of stakeholders — the general public, the media, staff, beneficiaries, government funders, individual donors, and more. Essentially, it speaks to everyone and no one in particular.

To do all of this, the tone of organizational messaging is often very formal, professional, and conservative.

As a result, organizational communications don't translate well to fundraising communications, and especially not to highly personal legacy giving messaging.

To understand these unique differences more clearly, we'll look at these contrasting characteristics:

Legacy Messaging	Organizational Messaging
More heartfelt & personal	More formal and generic
Uses plain language	Uses jargon/industry-speak
External focus	Inward organizational focus
Future focus	History focus

Legacy messaging is more heartfelt and personal vs. formal and generic

Every legacy donor is unique. And every legacy gift is highly personal to the individual making it. With legacy messaging — even when you are writing letter templates that will be used time and time again or videos for your website that anyone can watch — you want people to feel that you wrote these messages just for them, and that you are speaking right to their own heart.

An impersonal generic-feeling form letter just won't do. Neither will a corporate letter written in formal, passive voice: "We, here at ABC Charity...". It shouldn't come from more than one person, read like an academic paper, or worse, sound like a message "written by a lawyer in a Charles Dickens novel."

Legacy giving messaging uses
plain language vs. industry jargon

Most charities have brand guidelines and prescribed language around how they talk about their programs to ensure things are always described in the same way.

But sometimes, the wording can be overly stuck in sector jargon or use phrases like, "driving evidence-based innovation in X" or "with robust operational expansion in Y" that are more appropriate when seeking government grants, corporate sponsors, or recruiting staff.

The issue is that most industry-speak or business jargon phrases that sneak into your program descriptions or mission and vision statements are about what you do and how you do it.

But donors are giving because of why you do what you do and who or what benefits.

They give because of what you mean to our world.

And what you mean isn't complicated. I promise.

What you mean are things like:

- an opportunity to go to university for someone who never thought they'd get the chance,
- people will have support when natural disasters happen,
- vibrant arts and culture are accessible and thriving,
- a warm meal for someone who has no place to go,
- someday no one else will lose a loved one to a

given health issue, or,
- future generations grow up in a world with orcas.

When beginning to work with a new client, I often start by asking them to tell me a little about their organization. Most will tell me things like how many pairs of socks they gave out last year, or how many acres they protected, or how many different programs they run. They give me the numbers.

But what do those things mean? Why does giving out socks matter? Why is protecting those acres important? Why do those programs exist?

I call this channeling my inner three-year-old. Drilling down further and further by asking, why? Why? But, why? Keep asking "why" until you get to the answer underneath the surface of "what" and "how".

Ask yourself these "why?" questions about your own organization until you find the clear and obvious answers that would satisfy a three-year-old. Then you'll have the true essence of what you really mean to a legacy donor.

A note on reading levels
• • •
Legacy giving is simple — if we let it be.
We can express its essence in simple words.
We can share our vision clearly and concisely.
No matter how much you know your donors can
"handle" a more complex message — you want to keep
it simple. Why? Because a simple message is more
memorable, more accessible and feels more authentic.
The heart speaks in simple words.
So, keep your messaging around the grade 8 level
(or lower even) whenever possible.

Legacy messaging has an external focus vs. inward organizational focus

As I mentioned earlier, with organizational messaging, the focus is typically on the organization's credentials, its history, the founder, the programs, the achievements, the staff and the board.

For legacy messaging though, the focus is not on the organization itself.

Don't get me wrong, the organization is vital — it is the trusted partner working on the cause close to the donor's heart, and it will continue working to bring about a better world long after the donor themselves is gone.

But, legacy messaging focusses less on the organization and more on its impact in our world. It focusses on how donors can *make a difference in the world* with their legacy.

Legacy messaging is about the future vs. history

Often the aim of an organization's website, brochure, or other communications material is to demonstrate their credibility, using things like the founding story and a historical timeline of milestones. These pieces usually include mission, vision and values statements which are sometimes rather dated because creating new ones can be a big, time-consuming, and expensive endeavour.

A modest sprinkle of these elements can be useful in legacy messaging, but most of your legacy message should focus on the future rather than the past.

How legacy giving messaging is different from general fundraising messaging
---

Now let's look at how legacy messaging is different than other types of fundraising messaging.

We'll look at each of the following in more detail:

Legacy Messaging	General Fundraising Messaging
More broad	More specific
Achieve long-term vision	Meet current needs
Help future generations/ society	Help organization/ beneficiaries
More personal, private	More about social norms
Donor's beliefs, who they are	Worthiness of the cause
Soft ask, requires consideration	Urgent ask for immediate gift
Possible for anyone with assets	Requires available cash/ credit

Legacy giving is more broad vs. specific

We can't predict the future, so when we're talking to donors about legacy giving, we can't say for certain what the needs will be, what the best use of their legacy will be, or even whether the program they favour with their current giving will necessarily exist when their legacy gift is realized.

So, what do we do? We talk more broadly.

We talk about impact and values. We talk about what we mean to the community we serve, and our commitment to continue delivering that impact in future. And we talk about responding to the needs of the community well into the future, just as our organization has always done.

Often those coming from a more immediate giving background (annual, monthly, major giving) will feel nervous about leaving everything so open. They presume that donors will want to pin down deliverables and specifics — what should we say their gift will be used for? Should we offer a bunch of ways they can designate their gift to a preferred area?

Happily, for the most part, donors don't feel a need to be overly prescriptive about their legacy gift. These supporters have been connected to the organization for years, and they trust that you will make best use of their legacy to advance the cause they care about. So, keep your messaging simple, and talk about the impact they can have as broadly as possible.

As we learned in Chapter One — we want to avoid complicating a donor's decision with any additional layers of decision-making, so we don't find ourselves stuck in the jam paradox. The last thing you want to do with a donor who has decided to make a legacy gift is trigger decision paralysis about the myriad ways they could designate their gift. And your organization would much rather have an unrestricted gift anyway!

Supporters who do have something particular in mind will

talk to you about it, and these conversations are much better handled on a case-by-case basis anyway, so don't feel the need to broadcast designation options.

Legacy giving is about achieving a long-term vision vs. current needs

In annual appeals, we often get caught up in the pressing needs of today. To drive immediate gifts, we talk to donors about the current challenge: keeping the doors open and the lights on, replacing a piece of equipment with the latest and greatest, or a shortfall in a program's budget.

Immediate fundraising is in the trenches with the difficulties the organization and its beneficiaries face — but as a result, sometimes donors can end up feeling like they are constantly giving just to keep the organization they love afloat rather than moving the needle forward in a meaningful way.

And by overly placing the focus on current needs, budget shortfalls, and urgent struggles you risk making some donors question the organization's ongoing feasibility — which is the last thing you want them to be thinking about when they're considering a future gift.

Legacy giving messaging is about making progress toward achieving the big things the donor cares about. It is not about today's needs.

It requires a more optimistic and positive approach about what their legacy can do, and what you can achieve together in the future.

Legacy giving is about helping future generations vs. helping the organization or current beneficiaries

When talking to people about legacy giving, we generally want them to be imagining far into the future. What will the future hold in the next 50 or 100 years?

We use these long time horizons rather than say, the next 5 or 10 years, because no one wants to think that their legacy gift will be realized — in other words, *that they will die* — in the near future (even if that is potentially more realistic)!

This means you're not asking donors to support current beneficiaries or help the organization in the near-term. *You're talking about making the world a better place for the donor's children, grandchildren and the generations that come after.*

You are talking about more than making a gift to the organization. The organization is the facilitator, but the gift is ultimately to the world of the future.

Legacy giving is more personal and private vs. a social norm

Immediate giving is often quite public. You can be asked to make a charitable donation at the grocery store checkout, by your neighbour's child for their school fundraiser, by your employer offering payroll deduction matching, and countless other ways. This type of giving is often recognized publicly too. Donors' names are sometimes listed on charities' websites, in annual reports, or even put up on the wall as a form of recognition.

Legacy giving is much more private and personal. Because legacy giving is closely connected to one's own mortality (generally a taboo subject for the grocery store checkout!), people consider it a highly private topic. They're just not used to discussing it openly — sometimes not even with their own families!

It's also more rare. Only 5 to 8 percent of Canadians presently choose to create a legacy gift. It doesn't yet have the same level of acceptance and normalcy as immediate giving.

So, a lot of legacy giving marketing is designed to acclimatize people to the subject, and more firmly establish a social norm about creating a charitable legacy.

Thankfully, we can still market legacy giving in ways that honour people's desire for privacy about a highly personal decision. National awareness campaigns like Will Power in Canada and Remember a Charity in your Will in the UK, help promote legacy giving to the general public.

And, through a targeted approach, you can market these gifts directly to supporters, using things like legacy engagement surveys where people can self-identify as potential legacy donors. But, that's a topic for one of the future books in this five-part series!

Legacy giving is about a donor's beliefs and who they are vs. the worthiness of the cause

When people are asked to donate at a grocery store checkout counter the decision to give is usually about whether the cause is worthy, plus the expediency of giving, and a dash of social pressure.

The vast majority of people in Canada take part in some form of immediate giving each year. Statistics Canada's "Survey on Giving, Volunteering and Participating" consistently finds that between 72-82% of Canadians 25 years and older report giving to a charity or nonprofit.[7, 8] But this doesn't mean they necessarily have a deep personal connection to the cause — there is just a certain level of social obligation to put their spare change in the box at the checkout or buy a chocolate bar from their neighbour's kid.

What's that? You heard less than 20% of Canadians are giving to charity? [9, 10]

• • •

Every year, you may see panic-inducing posts and articles about how the number of Canadians giving to charity is plunging to frightening levels.

But most Canadians do give.

The falling figures you see quoted from the Canadian Revenue Agency are only counting income tax filers who get a tax receipt for their donation and claim it on their taxes.

The reality is — this undercounts a huge amount of giving.

People give to charity in all kinds of ways that don't qualify for a tax receipt.

And a lot of people forget to claim their charitable donations. For many, their giving isn't about reducing their taxes, so they don't bother to save the receipts or even care if they get one.

That's why I quote Statistics Canada rather than the CRA numbers. It's more inclusive of all the different ways people give these days — because how and where Canadians are giving may have shifted — but most do still give!

People give to many, many different causes in their lifetime — some they care deeply about, and others they contribute to because "that's just what we do" in our society — but they only have one chance to make a final statement about the causes they care about with their legacy.

So, the importance of a legacy gift is heightened. The meaning of that gift is heightened. And they often reveal a person's innermost values.

Legacy giving requires a soft ask and time for consideration vs. urgency

It's a basic tenet of fundraising communications that for immediate giving you want people to feel they need to give, well, immediately. You'll often see messaging that includes things like: "Give now!", "Make your gift today!". The messaging includes a deadline for the appeal that is highlighted with increasing urgency in reminders as the date draws near. For immediate giving, this works. It creates a sense of pressure that the donor wants to alleviate, it helps people decide to make the gift right away rather than putting it off and potentially getting distracted or forgetting, and it gets cash in the door right away.

But for legacy giving, you need a different approach.

Why? Well, for most donors, it generally takes *2 to 3 years* to go from considering a gift to having a gift written into their Will.

Wills get written or updated when the time is right for the donor, based on circumstances in their own life — like a marriage or divorce, the birth of a child or grandchild, or a health scare. Donors don't create or update their Will just because we ask them to make a legacy gift.

Rather than saying "Create your legacy today!" or "Make a gift in your Will now!", what works best is to ask people to "Consider creating a gift in your Will." This soft ask acknowledges that people generally need to reflect on their decision, and that you're not expecting them to know what they want their legacy to look like right away.

But immediate action is now more possible

• • •

One exciting trend in legacy giving is that it's now possible for us to help supporters more immediately go from getting inspired about their legacy to taking action.

With online Will-writing tools like Willfora and others, supporters can go from getting excited about the impact of a legacy gift to your organization to writing a gift in their Will with the click of a button.

People will still typically need time to think through their legacy, and an online tool isn't a fit for every donor's needs — but by creating a series of communications that inspire, and offering the option to create their Will within minutes for free — we can narrow the gap between a donor's initial interest in legacy giving and having them put a gift in their Will for a cause they care about.

Applying pressure or pushing people to decide sooner than they are ready is more likely to backfire than it is to speed the process along.

If anything, you want to reassure people that it is natural to take their time with a big decision, and that you know deciding how best to create their legacy is important and meaningful to them. You want to be careful to avoid giving people the impression that if they don't know right away if legacy giving is right for them, or if they don't feel it is as easy to do as someone else, that they are not a fit for this type of gift.

Our approach should be sensitive to this — and give the donor time and space to consider without any pressure. At the same time, find ways to stay top of mind with the supporter so that when the time is right for them to write, or update, their Will, they are still thinking of you and inspired about what a legacy gift to your organization can do.

Legacy giving is possible for anyone with assets vs. those with available cashflow

One of the things I find most beautiful about legacy giving is that it really is possible for ordinary people to make a big impact.

Most supporters cannot make a five- or six-figure gift during their lifetime. They may have everyday expenses that take up much of their current earnings, or, after retirement they may be on a fixed income.

However, legacy giving is possible for anyone with assets. If the supporter owns a house, has investments, or built up their retirement savings accounts, these assets can help them to make a gift through their estate.

You may have heard stories about legacy gifts that catch

organizations by surprise because they suddenly get a very large legacy gift from someone who gave small amounts annually.

This is partly because for a long time, we thought good candidates for potential legacy gifts would be similar to a major gift donor. It was assumed that those most likely to consider a legacy gift would be the wealthy — because they tend to be more well-versed with a variety of financial vehicles and are more likely to be looking to minimize the amount of taxes they owe.

This is another hold-over of the financial planning approach to legacy giving — the logical, prudency-focused approach that we talked about in Chapter One.

And while it is absolutely worth approaching high-net-worth donors about adding a legacy gift into their philanthropic mix — what we see time and time again is that a supporter's ability to give during their lifetime often has nothing to do with how likely they are to consider a legacy gift.

A donor who has been giving for 20 years and has no children may only give $10 a year, but they could have an estate worth much more and no natural beneficiaries. Plus, a donor who has been giving regularly for many years is far more likely to create a legacy gift.

Legacy giving is about connection. And when you prioritize this in your messaging, you'll resonate with those who care — whatever the size of their bank account. This means you will ultimately capture the attention of both groups — those who can give a lot during their lifetime, and those who give less annually but can make an impact with their legacy.

With all of this in mind, we can really see just how different legacy giving messaging is from the other kinds of communications you may be creating for your organization.

In Chapter Four, we'll look at how we can most effectively engage your supporters in considering a legacy gift by using key messages in your legacy program.

ENGAGE AND APPLY

1. If you have legacy material for your organization, have a look at it. Is there anything you would change based on what has been discussed so far?

2. If you don't currently have legacy giving material at your organization, take a look at your general organizational messaging. What things might translate well to a legacy message? Which things would you need to adjust to resonate more with a legacy audience?

COMMUNICATE CLEARLY
WITH A LEGACY KEY MESSAGE

Investing the time to create a clear and compelling legacy key message makes your legacy marketing more powerful, because the message will become deeply planted in supporters' minds through repetition. A consistent message makes your legacy program more cohesive. And it makes creating all of your future legacy material faster.

But what is a key message and why should you have a separate one for your legacy giving program?

What is a
key message?

You can think of a key message as a guiding beacon, illuminating the path for your supporters through a sea of information in the noisy world of fundraising. It is the core idea that defines your organization and tells your audience who you are. A powerful key message helps your organization stand out and be memorable in the minds of your supporters.

Put more plainly, *a key message is an important idea that you want your audience to hear, easily understand, and then remember.*

If you think about it, this is how we operate in our everyday lives. We are attracted to, and more likely to remember, things that are significant to us and that are communicated clearly. If you've ever met someone who likes to expound on the technical complexities of their job, or their favourite sport that you know nothing about, or a TV show you don't watch — you know the agony of having a firehose of immaterial information come your way. Most likely, you tune out and can't remember the details later because it wasn't relevant or interesting to you.

On the other hand, when you meet someone who talks about things that you care about, and they discuss them in a way that is easy to understand, you are naturally more engaged. You may discover shared interests and ideas. They may speak with passion and emotion that draws you in. You are likely going to listen more attentively and remember what is said. You may even ask questions because you want to hear more. That's how you want your supporters — and potential supporters — to feel when they hear your key message.

In fundraising, we typically go one step further. We want a fundraising key message to be something that supporters hear, understand, remember, and *act on*.

A good fundraising key message creates meaning and resonance with donors, then inspires them to take action and make an impact.

A key message should be fluid, persuasive, and motivating. It should be simple to say and understand, and it should be able to serve as a "sound bite" or "elevator pitch" that captures supporters' attention and encourages further engagement.

A key message is not the same as your organization's tagline, which aims to encapsulate your organization in just a few words (usually 3 to 8). A key message is more in-depth. You want to be able to say it in roughly 30 seconds. Written out, it should ideally be one to three sentences.

A key message should be clear, concise, relevant, compelling, memorable, and authentic.

It should not be full of buzzwords, jargon, or overly formal language. And it shouldn't be set in stone!

Typically, organizations will have an overarching key message, and secondary key messages about specific programs. These secondary key messages can be for the programs you provide in the community and for internal programs like your legacy giving program.

A key message is a good way to ensure that the most vital, compelling information is at the centre of all your communications — keeping that message consistent over time and across different materials, content creators, and channels.

Key message
characteristics
—

When you're creating a great key message, whether it's for your organization as a whole, or your legacy giving program specifically, keep the five following characteristics in mind:

CLARITY: A clear key message is concise, easy to understand and aims to communicate the essence of your organization in a way that your target audience can quickly grasp. A good key message uses simple words, short sentences, and straightforward grammar to ensure the message is clear.

> *"The single biggest problem in communication is the illusion that it has taken place."*
> *– George Bernard Shaw*

> *"Whatever words we utter should be chosen with care for people will hear them and be influenced by them for good or ill."*
> *– Buddha*

CONSISTENCY: A consistent key message reinforces your organization's position, meaning, and the impact you have in the world. Seeing the same message repeated over time creates trust and a strong foundation for long-term donor loyalty. More importantly, by consistently delivering your key message across various communication channels and touchpoints, you begin to embed your message more deeply in the minds of supporters.

> *Repetition, repetition, repetition*
> • • •
> *Frank Luntz, a political communications consultant, and author of Words That Work says,*

"Here's a simple rule: You say it again, and you say it again, and you say it again, and you say it again, and you say it again, and then again and again and again and again, and about the time that you're absolutely sick of saying it is about the time that your target audience has heard it for the first time."

Winston Churchill would agree. He said: "If you have an important point to make, don't try to be subtle or clever. Use a pile driver. Hit the point once. Then come back and hit it again. Then hit it a third time — a tremendous whack."

RELEVANCE: A good key message should feel suited to your audience as if it was tailor-made for them. You want to demonstrate that you understand their values and goals, and that together, you are working towards a shared vision. By creating a highly relevant key message you increase the likelihood that supporters will think of you when they want to make a gift that they find meaningful. By showing supporters how aligned you are — and demonstrating your shared values — you create a stronger connection.

"It is through the strength of what is genuine that meaningful connections build into relationships."
– Michelle Tillis Lederman

"Being heard and understood is one of the greatest desires of the human heart."
– Richard Carlson

EMOTIONAL IMPACT: A powerful key message resonates with your supporters' emotions. It goes beyond logical reasoning and engages with their hearts. A key message that connects emotionally with your supporters is like a warm hug that makes them feel understood and valued. As Dr. Jen Shang's research shows, you can, in fact, provide donors with a sense of well-being. By fostering a deep emotional connection between your donors and your organization, you increase their sense of attachment and alignment with your work.

"Communication is the transfer of emotion."
– Seth Godin

"I've learned that people will forget what you said, people will forget what you did, but people will never forget how you made them feel."
– Dr. Maya Angelou

DISTINCTIVENESS: You also want to differentiate your organization from other nonprofits. Your key message should highlight what makes you stand out from others that do similar work. By emphasizing your unique impact on the things that matter to them, you differentiate yourself and create a memorable impression for donors.

"What makes you different or weird —
that's your strength."
– Meryl Streep

"If you don't distinguish yourself from the crowd, you'll just be the crowd."
– Rebecca Mark

What is a legacy key message?

A legacy key message is not as broad as your overarching organizational key message. It highlights the impact of legacy giving and aims to encourage and inspire people to consider a legacy gift.

If you only remember one thing about legacy key messages, let it be this: *Your legacy key message should focus on why people create legacy gifts, rather than how.*

People create legacy gifts for charity because they share the organization's vision — so much so that they want to help make it a reality for future generations.

By developing a powerful and compelling legacy key message, you will succinctly communicate the importance of legacy giving, the impact a legacy can have, and inspire supporters to consider including your organization as part of their personal legacy.

The goal of your legacy key message is to capture the attention — and the hearts — of supporters, and to inspire them to consider making a legacy gift to your organization. And of course, just as with your overarching key message, your legacy message should be clear, concise, consistent, emotionally appealing, relevant, and distinctive.

Ideally, your legacy key message succinctly conveys the essence of how legacies can make a difference. It should have a future-focused perspective and highlight the positive and aspirational aspects of this kind of gift. By connecting with the hearts of supporters — and tapping into their visualized autobiography as we discussed in Chapter Two — a legacy key message creates an emotional connection, inspiring them to make a legacy gift not only as part of their philanthropic journey, but ultimately, their life story.

Finally, don't forget that an effective key message also *includes an ask to prompt supporters to consider a legacy gift.* This is one of the most vital elements of a legacy key message, and yet, it is also the thing I most often see left out of legacy giving communications.

Why have a legacy key message?

Having a well-crafted legacy key message is vital for your legacy program for several reasons.

The first, and most obvious, is that by having a clear and memorable legacy key message, you ensure supporters understand the potential impact and importance of legacy giving. Your key message serves as the mainstay of your legacy messaging, inspiring supporters to consider creating a lasting legacy for the cause they care about. It also serves as a touchstone for all future legacy program communications, ensuring that the significance of legacy giving is shared consistently and integrated into other initiatives and campaigns. This continuity creates a consistent and cohesive donor experience, solidifying for supporters why legacy gifts are so meaningful and in alignment with their values.

A legacy key message also provides a unified way to communicate the importance of this kind of gift within your organization and ensures that everyone is singing from the same songbook. It makes it easy for your entire team — whether they are fundraisers or not — to understand how important this kind of gift is for your organization — and be able to see the value of it.

Not everyone within your organization will speak about legacy giving regularly. But, having a legacy key message gives board members, senior leadership, and ideally your entire team — whether they deliver your frontline programs, answer the phone, or meet with donors — the language and confidence to talk in simple terms about legacy giving as a potential way to support your future work. It removes hesitations and fears of getting it wrong, allowing for more effective and consistent conversations with potential legacy donors, and can help everyone in your organization recognize when people may be interested in this type of gift.

Why everyone in your organization
should know about legacy giving
• • •
It pains me to say, but I've come across multiple
organizations over the years who have lost out on legacy gifts
because someone in their organization didn't understand legacy
giving. I've heard of donors who called to ask about "bequests",
or who asked if they could speak to someone who could
help them with making a gift in their Will, and were told,
"I don't think we do that."

The moral of the story is — make sure everyone
in your organization knows how important legacy giving
is, what questions people may ask, and who to
direct those enquiries to.

Lastly, you want a well-defined legacy key message so you can more easily incorporate the legacy ask into your various communication touchpoints, and across multiple platforms. This integrated approach ensures that supporters will repeatedly see and clearly understand the invitation to consider leaving a legacy gift — and hopefully, when the time is right for them, be inspired to take action.

Whether it is used during in-person conversations, a legacy video, your monthly newsletter, or annual impact reports, having a formalized legacy key message allows for widespread and consistent messaging, and you won't have to reinvent the wheel each time.

Where do you use a legacy key message?

Well, ideally — everywhere! Any way that you communicate with supporters is a great place to integrate a legacy message.

WEBSITE — Feature legacy giving as an important way to consider making a gift on your website's donation page or on a dedicated legacy giving section to engage and inspire potential legacy donors. When organizations start to see the benefit of legacy giving, they sometimes also choose to feature a banner image during certain times like Make a Will Week in Canada (varies by province) or Leave a Legacy Month (May).

APPEALS — On your reply device, replace the tick box where supporters can ask for more information about legacy giving with a tick box where supporters can say *they're inspired to hear more about how their legacy can make a difference.* If your appeals are segmented, you can speak to legacy expectants about their legacy, or to prospective legacy donors about the fact that they're considering a legacy gift, right in the appeal letter itself — and this actually increases annual giving too!

CASE FOR SUPPORT — Incorporate the legacy key message into your organization's overall case for support, highlighting the importance of legacy giving and the unique impact it can have on your mission. You can also create a standalone legacy case for support to demonstrate the impact of legacy gifts more fully and encourage more supporters to include you as part of their legacy.

NEWSLETTER ARTICLES – Include the legacy key message in articles or stories that highlight the impact of legacy giving and demonstrate the value and benefits of creating a lasting legacy. You can also tell an impact story that isn't legacy-related, so long as you make the connection to legacy giving for donors. E.g., "Create [more of the impact shared in the story] with your legacy."

DONOR CONVERSATIONS – When engaging in one-on-one conversations with potential legacy donors, incorporate the legacy key message to convey the emotional essence of creating a lasting impact and inspire them to take action.

VOICEMAIL MESSAGE – Include the legacy key message in your recorded voicemail message, serving as a succinct reminder for callers about the significance of creating a legacy and encouraging them to explore legacy giving opportunities.

EMAIL SIGNATURE – Incorporate the legacy key message into your staff email signatures, providing a consistent and subtle reminder of the importance of legacy giving across all email communications both internal and external — and don't forget to include the link to your legacy webpage.

VIDEOS – Create videos that highlight the power of legacy giving and feature the legacy key message as a central component. These videos can be shared on social media, your website, and at fundraising events to inspire supporters to consider making a lasting impact. You can even include a link to the video in your email signature too!

E-BLASTS – Send out targeted e-appeals dedicated to legacy giving, using the legacy key message to effectively communicate the transformative possibilities and benefits of leaving a legacy.

SUPPORTER SURVEYS – Integrate the legacy key message and related questions into supporter surveys to generate interest in legacy giving and identify those who've already left a gift.

ANNUAL / IMPACT / STEWARDSHIP REPORTS – Incorporate the legacy key message into your organization's annual, impact, or stewardship reports to demonstrate the long-term impact of legacy gifts and the importance of legacy giving within your organization's overall achievements and goals.

SOCIAL MEDIA POSTS – Craft social media posts that showcase the impact of legacy giving using the legacy key message. This helps spread awareness and engages your online community in the conversation around creating a lasting legacy.

PAID SEARCH AND ADS – Whether through Google, or social media platforms, budgeting for paid ads can help your legacy message reach a much wider audience. Make use of the available grants to non-profits to maximize your budget for ads.

EVENTS AND PRESENTATIONS — Use the legacy key message in speeches, presentations, and event materials to consistently communicate the importance of legacy giving and inspire attendees to consider making a legacy gift.

By incorporating your legacy key message into multiple communication channels, you can effectively plant the seed of legacy giving with supporters many times over the course of a year, ensuring the message cuts through the noise. You'll also be more likely to stay top of mind with people who are in the process of considering a legacy gift — so they remain inspired and are still thinking about you when it comes time for them to create their Will.

What do we want our legacy key message to say?

Your legacy message should convey a few important things:

1. Clearly express the ***vision*** of a better future your organization and its supporters are united in trying to achieve.
2. Reflect the ***values, beliefs, and impacts*** that are associated with your organization so that donors who share those values and beliefs identify more deeply with your organization.
3. ***Demonstrate how important legacy gifts are for moving the vision forward,***
4. And ***make the ask!***

Sounds easy, right?

If you're saying, "But Aimée, we already put our Mission, Vision, and Values statements on our website, and in our legacy brochure and annual report, and..."

Let me just pause to say, the mission, vision, and values on an organization's website are often outdated, jargon-filled statements created by committee about honesty, integrity, and teamwork that should be absolute givens, and they may say nothing about what you actually mean in the world or how you are different from any other organization that works in your sector.

So sometimes, you'll need to dig down to find the real values and vision you need to be communicating to get to the heart of what your donors are resonating with.

So, how do we do this? How do we share our organization's vision, values, what we believe, what we think the future can look like, and the impact a legacy can have for generations to come?

How can we do this in ways that feel natural, that can work in conversation or in writing — both in mass-produced print pieces like a legacy brochure, but also in social media, or your legacy webpage?

How can it still feel authentic throughout the long timeframe most people need when they are considering a legacy gift — often 2–3 years?

And how can we do this without falling into any of the pitfalls of giving too much information, or triggering death-reminder avoidance issues?

We'll cover all this and more in the next two chapters as

we take a closer look at the building blocks of legacy key messages and then start putting them all together.

ENGAGE AND APPLY

1. Can you identify an overarching key message that your organization uses regularly?

2. Do you have any key messages about your organization's specific programs — either service delivery programs or internal programs like major giving or monthly giving? If yes, how and where are these currently being used?

3. Do you already have a legacy key message? If you do, does it deliver on each of the five characteristics discussed — clarity, consistency, relevance, emotional impact, and distinctiveness? Are there any things you would change to make it better?

4. How can you integrate your legacy key message across different communication channels? Think about any existing touchpoints where you communicate with supporters, such as your website, newsletters, social media, and donor conversations.

THE BUILDING BLOCKS OF A
COMPELLING LEGACY KEY MESSAGE

_____

By this point, hopefully, you are sold on the value of having a legacy key message and are now thinking about the long list of places you can integrate your legacy message once you've created it. This brings us to our next step — helping you build a great legacy key message.

I often think of this phase in two ways:

1. Like I'm cooking — gathering my ingredients so I have everything I need — which once combined

will become something far greater than the sum of its parts, and,

2. Like I'm solving a jigsaw puzzle — making sure I have all the pieces, getting a sense of the big picture on the front of the puzzle box, and then fitting it all together.

So, let's talk about the components — whether you think of them as recipe ingredients or puzzle pieces — what should you include in your legacy key message?

What makes a great key message?

First, let's think more deeply about some of the aspects of a great message that will help your supporters feel engaged:

- Vision
- Values
- Impact
- People and places
- Conversational language
- Inspiration, not education
- A clear next step

Vision

Taking a page from Frank Luntz, I'll use repetition to help drive home a key point. In most cases, **at the heart of legacy giving is a shared vision of a better future that you and your supporters both wish to achieve.**

It is possibly the most essential ingredient.

Your vision must be in your key message — it is the "Why?". It is what most inspires supporters to create a legacy, and it is what will take shape in the supporter's visualized auto-biography. Paint a picture of that better world. Help them imagine it coming about. Let them see how their legacy can be a part of making it happen. Your vision is aspirational, motivational, and compelling to those who want to leave the world a little better for future generations.

Remember, the vision you talk about may not be your organization's official vision statement, which may have been crafted decades ago, and include outdated language, jargon, or are just not very bold.

Instead, you should think about what it would mean to the world if your organization achieved its purpose and actually solved the issues you work to address. What does that future look like? How are people's lives improved? What would it mean for future generations?

It is that better future vision that you want to convey to supporters.

Values

Another common reason people create legacy gifts is because their own beliefs and values align with the organization's, and they want to support those values continuing in the world after they are gone.

Again, we're not necessarily talking about the values on your website that may say things like honesty, teamwork, and respect. It should go without saying that organizations uphold those values, yet they are some of the most common words in organizational values statements along with integrity, accountability, and trust. Because these are such givens, you're not really telling people anything about what you stand for.

We're talking about the values demonstrated in your work, the reason you exist, and what you value beyond the baseline qualities all well-run organizations possess.

This may be values like caring for others, protecting animals or the environment, access to education, or human rights. But they may also be more ineffable values, like hope, compassion, justice, or faith.

Faith-based organizations are some of the most successful I've ever come across in legacy giving. This is likely for a few reasons, but I believe one of them is because they regularly talk about their values. Whether in Christian tradition, Judaism, Hinduism, Buddhism or other faiths, there are commonly known core virtues or values which are well-defined and widely held.

For secular organizations, the challenge is to define and regularly integrate your values into your messaging. You want your audience to have a good grasp of what you mean and what you stand for.

Your values should ideally show up throughout your broad communications. And, with your legacy key message, you have an opportunity to reaffirm these values so donors can see how your organization's values are aligned with their own.

Impact

Though your legacy donors will never get to see the impact their gift will have, you still want to give them a sense of the scale of what their legacy gift can help achieve.

Legacy gifts are often the largest and most meaningful gifts people will ever make. This is especially true for those who usually give $10, $25, or $50 dollars a year. The impact of their legacy gift may be far greater than they've ever imagined before.

To help your supporters understand the significance of legacy gifts, paint them a picture of the long-term impact so they can imagine it as part of their life's story — so they can see themselves living on in some way through the future work of your organization.

Of course, you don't know what the impact of your audience of supporters' gifts will be — they will (hopefully) be realized years in the future and will vary in size. So how do you speak about the impact of their legacy gift?

You speak broadly, but compellingly. Talk about what legacy gifts you've received in the past have helped to accomplish. Talk about how legacy gifts you're receiving today are having a meaningful impact on your work. Talk about what legacy gifts can do.

You may also talk about the level of contribution legacy giving makes to your overall revenue pool. Usually this would be in supplemental text and not directly in your key message, except potentially in the broadest sense, like saying, "Legacy gifts can help provide vital, stable funding for x, y, z."

Will talking about impact mean we receive
more restricted legacy gifts?

• • •

Sometimes, there's a concern that if you highlight any of the
potential impacts of legacy giving, supporters may
be more inclined to designate that their gift fund a specific
program or area of your work. This is generally not the case,
especially if you make sure to give people a sense of
the variety of things that legacy gifts can do, without
overpromising what a supporter's gift will do.

Throughout your other legacy material, position the idea that
flexibility helps their legacy gift provide the most benefit for the
most important priorities at the time a gift is realized.
And, of course, the sample wording you provide for gifts in
Wills should aim to leave things as open as possible.

I often see organizations too prominently featuring wording
for designated gifts. This can make people believe they
should designate their gift. So rather than widely publicizing
gift designation wording, make it available upon request, so
you can have that conversation with supporters one-on-one.
This helps ensure that you can actually fulfill the
intention of their gift's designation, too!

Though all this good stuff about impact can't necessarily
make it into a tight legacy key message — it can be your
leaping-off point. So, speak to the tremendous importance
of legacy gifts for your organization and speak to the big-
picture impact people can have by making your organization
part of their legacy plans.

People and places

Do you ever find yourself seeing a face in the bark of a tree, an
oddly shaped fruit, or a cloud? Most people do. It's because

our brains are wired to see faces. Right from the moment we're born, the first things we see — before our vision is even fully developed — are faces. Our parents' faces, our grand-parents' faces, our caregivers' faces. We are born with this ability and instinct to orient toward people, and in as little as a few days, we begin to recognize and seek connection from others. We are social creatures — even us introverts! — and we have an ingrained desire to care about one another.

So, talk about the people you help.

- Who are they? Kids, youth, seniors, neighbours, community members, people in an emergency situation?
- Avoid letting their circumstances overshadow their humanity. Avoid describing people as cancer sufferers, parolees, flood victims, etc. These people are our neighbours, children, and fellow citizens who are facing difficulty, but it is not their identity; it is not who they are.
- Remember to describe them in future-oriented terms when possible — e.g., "future generations", "tomorrow's youth", "people in the years to come", etc.

Talk about your supporters too.

- Who are they? Community members, engaged volunteers, advocates, partners in facing a particular issue, etc.
- Include some of the key words Dr. Jen Shang's findings show are most used to describe a moral identity:

- Caring
- Compassionate
- Kind

- Fair
- Friendly
- Generous

- Helpful
- Hardworking
- Trustworthy

In my first or second year working in legacy giving,
someone said something along the lines of,
"Well, sure, if we helped sad puppies or sick kids,
legacy giving would be easier."

There is an idea out there that some causes are not as
attractive or capable of generating interest in legacy giving.

I think it is probably true that some causes are easier
to market to the general public — videos of sad dog eyes
accompanied by Sarah McLachlan music does a lot
for new donor acquisition for sure.

But legacy giving isn't about attracting new people to your cause
— you have the benefit of preaching to the converted!
Ninety-nine times out of a hundred, legacy donors come from
within your donor base. They already support your work.
They already care about your mission. They've likely been
giving for years. In my experience, it's generally just a matter
of doing the work to actively promote legacy giving to those
who already care, and then making the ask.

Most of us also have strong connections to places. It is one of
the key donor identities named in Dr. Jen Shang's research.
For some people, it is their neighbourhood; for others
their city or hometown; and still others their country or an
international attachment. By reminding people of your
impact in the area that is important to them — whether it is
at a community, regional, national, or international level —
your key message helps prime this important identity every
time they see it.

Talk about where you work, and what your reach is.

- Reference geography if it is a fit — your community's name, region, or country. For example, "Helping [community name] thrive" or "Ensuring people across [region] have access to…"
- Reference more generic reach terms — "Fostering [value] in our community", "Conserving our nation's wild spaces", "Global impact", etc.

Conversational language

I've already shared my first rule of writing for humans — "When writing for humans, write like a human."

But what does this really mean in practice?

It means:

- talk like a person, not like an organization.
- your message shouldn't be a vocabulary test.
- get rid of jargon and sector-insider terms.
- if you break out a thesaurus, it's to find a simpler word, not a more complex one.
- a kid in grade 8 should easily understand it.
- when you try saying it out loud, it sounds the same as how you really talk.

The aim is to have your message feel natural. Human. Authentic.

Saying it out loud is a genuinely great test. Are you tripping over it in places? Are any sentences so long you're gasping for breath? Does any of it sound false or overly flowery?

After you've said it out loud to yourself a few times, try saying it to others — people within your organization and those who really don't know much about it at all. Ask them: Do they get it? Is there anything they don't understand? Is there anything that sounds phoney?

Then talk to these same people again a few days later — what do they remember about your key message? Can they recall the most important points? Are there any words or phrases that they found memorable?

It's a hard test. Because as we know, people often need to hear a message many times before it sinks in. But this can give you good clues about what stands out, whether people really get it, and how memorable your message is.

One way to make your message more memorable is to embed your key message within stories. Humans are hardwired to remember stories. In fact, you are 20x more likely to remember a fact if it's tied to a story.

Why? Stories evoke images and emotions. Visualization and emotional connection activate more parts of our brains. And memories stored with more active connections in our brains are more easily recalled.

Put another way? We remember what we feel.

Inspiration, not education

Albert Einstein once said, "Imagination is more important than knowledge. Knowledge is limited, imagination encircles the world."

I'm going to take a great liberty (hopefully Albert won't mind), and paraphrase this for our legacy-giving purposes to say: "Inspiration is more important than education. Educating can feel patronizing, while inspiring can motivate the world."

Don't get me wrong, I love learning. I think education is great — when you're learning something new.

But when someone assumes you don't know something and tells you things you already know as if they're doing you a favour — well, that just tends to rub people the wrong way.

And, as of 2019, 86% of Canadians *already know* they can make a charitable gift in their Will.[11]

That means the vast majority of donors already know they can make a gift in their Will to charity. And since nearly 90% of people will have a Will by the age of 75 — you don't need to waste time or energy "educating" them on why they should have one. So don't be a planned-giving*splainer!*

Try to weed out words like "learn", "information", "guide", and other education-focused words from your legacy giving messaging. These types of words set up the dynamic that your organization is the teacher, and the donor is uneducated.

Instead, remember that legacy giving comes from within. Just focus on inspiring the part of people that already cares — and already has the knowledge — to get them to take action.

Really? You don't talk about tax savings?

•••

At this initial messaging stage, I don't — for two reasons.

1) Saving tax isn't the reason most people give — it is just the cherry on top of their main reason. If I'm working with an organization that already features tax savings information prominently, I include a small blurb about how legacy gifts can also mean a reduction in their estate's final tax return. If I'm working with an organization that hasn't featured tax information, I don't actively lead with this message.

I strongly suspect that when people who are surveyed say that tax savings is the reason they are making a legacy gift, it is in no small part because we have told people that is the main reason to do it for decades! They're just saying what they learned from us.

It's a chicken-and-egg situation that we've created for ourselves. That said, leading with a values-based message and then adding that tax-saving cherry on top in follow-up messaging can help someone who is on the fence about a legacy gift decide to go for it. But I always lead with vision and values to initially pique interest.

2) To get on my soapbox for a moment, the other reason I don't talk about tax savings is because I think our society is worse off when people hear over and over again that paying taxes is bad.

So many organizations like food banks, libraries, hospitals, and others are having to work harder to fundraise because governments keep cutting funding for services that they used to provide for. Nonprofits keep trying to fill this growing gap — but it puts much more pressure on organizations, especially small nonprofits or those who work with underserved communities. Time and time again, it is shown that these organizations do not receive a proportional amount of funding from donors, which perpetuates systemic injustices. And the more we tell people they should try to avoid taxes, the more we spiral the entire system downwards.

A clear next step

Can you imagine if recipes were just a list of ingredients and then you had to figure out what to do with them? I don't know about you, but most of my baking wouldn't turn out like the picture.

That's pretty much what a legacy key message without a clear call to action is like. Yes, there may be some people will figure it out and make the gift you haven't explicitly asked for.

But in fundraising, as we know, *you have to ask in order to receive.*

If you create a great key message about the amazing work you can accomplish with legacy gifts, but then don't make the ask, well, it just feels like an informational blurb to most people. It enters the realm of "That's nice to know," instead of "This is something I should consider doing."

It's important to be clear about what you want your legacy giving message to do, so that later, you can assess whether it is successful.

- Are you developing initial awareness about legacy giving among supporters?
- Are you building a pipeline of warm leads who would consider a gift?
- Are you actively trying to drive new legacy gift commitments?

Whatever the purpose, you need to help people directly make the connection to themselves by asking them to consider a legacy gift.

Notice something?

• • •

You may have noticed that I always say, "consider a legacy gift", or "create" or "make" or "include" a legacy gift. But I never say, "leave a legacy gift". Why?

I bet by now you can guess — it's because that pesky word "leave" can inadvertently trigger thoughts of mortality and death. We want to keep the focus on the creation phase of their gift, not the time the gift is realized when they leave this mortal coil.

Remember — you don't need to push too hard. And you may also want to preface the ask with language like, "after you have provided for your loved ones…". It reassures people that you're not asking them to sacrifice their family's needs, and it shows them that you recognize family comes first.

Our board doesn't think it is appropriate to ask people about a legacy gift — what should we do?

• • •

Oh, how I wish I didn't hear this so often from organizations. And while it's less common today than even 5 years ago, there is still this resistance, from some quarters, to making a direct ask. It's most often bound up in death-avoidance behaviours, and in the idea that anything related to death is too private and taboo to discuss. But we're not talking about death. We're talking about making an impact. We're talking about meaning, and values, and things people generally feel good about in life.

My recommendation? First, share the average value of legacy gifts to your organization, or the average in your area. For example, in Canada the nationwide average is $35,000, but is much higher — even double that figure — in urban areas. Help them understand the scale of the impact each legacy gift has. Then, show them examples of organizations that have good legacy messaging that includes an ask so they can see it doesn't *need to be scary or prying. And lastly, suggest doing a trial run to test including a legacy ask in your messaging. You could do some A/B testing with a legacy piece that has an ask vs. no ask and see which one gets more response. Or you could update the legacy messaging on your website to include an ask (since it's easy to change back) and see if the phones ring off the hook with outraged calls from upset donors. (Spoiler alert: they won't!)*

Recipe for a great legacy key message
• • •

Ingredients
Vision + values + impact, impact, impact + the people and places that matter + the ask!

Steps
1. Combine all ingredients carefully using compelling, accessible language and a conversational tone.
2. Serve on its own, or with engaging stories for greater retention among supporters.

ENGAGE AND APPLY

1. Reflecting on the core purpose and values that drive your organization, what words stand out to you that are in your organization's current mission, vision, and values statements? Are any important words missing?

2. When you talk to supporters, what are some common themes or words they use to describe why they give to your organization? How do they describe the better future they're trying to achieve? What does it mean to them?

3. What are the beliefs or values that underlie the desire to achieve this better future? Are there emotions that go along with those beliefs?

4. If the better future is achieved, what would be the impact? What are the benefits? Are there specific ways that legacy gifts help deliver this impact?

5. Who benefits from the vision being achieved?

6. What is the next step for the donor? Why should they do it now?

PUTTING IT ALL TOGETHER —
CREATING YOUR LEGACY KEY MESSAGE,
TAGLINE, WORDMARK & BRAND

Now the time has come!

We've talked about some of the pitfalls of traditional planned giving messaging, we've talked about how we can think about this differently and we've talked about the ways legacy giving messaging is different from general organizational messaging and other fundraising communications.

We've talked about the importance of key messages and why

you want to have a legacy key message, and finally, we talked about the essential ingredients for a great legacy message.

All we have left to do — is actually do it! So, let's write some legacy key messages, shall we?

Three methods for creating a legacy key message

If you look up how to create a key message on the internet, you'll find all sorts of ways people like to approach this. We'll go through three different options, and you can choose the one that works best for you and your organization.

I. The traditional method

This first method is commonly used in business but can work for nonprofits too.

The basic formula for creating a key message with this method is:

Core message + Supporting Statement(s) + Proof

Of course, in fundraising, we're going to add an ask at the end so it's:

Core Message + Supporting Statement(s) + Proof + Ask

Let's see how this might work for a small hospital foundation:

ABC Hospital is a leader in health care today, and you can help keep it that way for generations to come. *[Core Message]* Now, you and your loved ones — from newborns to seniors — can receive care right here in our community. *[Supporting Statement]* Together, we're living longer, and enjoying more health than ever before. *[Proof]* Let's ensure future generations can say the same — please, consider a gift in your Will to ABC Hospital Foundation. *[Ask]*

Not bad. In the first sentence we're positioning the organization as a leader in the sector, we're planting the seed that there's a way they can help keep it that way, and we're priming people to be thinking of the long-term future. We then demonstrate why this should be important to them and what it means to others. And, while the example says, "in our community" alternatively you could choose to prime people's geographic identity by saying "in [town name]." Next, we state the impact as proof. This proof could be something more tangible, like how many visitors the hospital sees in a year for example, but we've gone for a broader, more feel-good impact here. Finally, we close with an ask to consider a gift in their Will.

In practice, and as you can see in this example, this method can get a little wordy, particularly if you want to offer multiple supporting statements or points of proof. You might opt to use bullet points for some of the support and proof statements to keep things a little tighter.

All in all, however, a solid statement. But too long for usage in your email signature or your voicemail message.

So, let's look at a model that prioritizes brevity.

2. The 27/9/3 format

This method is a favourite for crisis communications. The message is super concise and aims to be very focused, easily repeatable, and highly memorable.

The 27/9/3 format takes its name from its very prescriptive formula — the message must be 27 words or less, take no longer than 9 seconds to say, and include no more than 3 points.

If you like writing to a word count, this method is kind of fun. If you struggle to keep your bio to 100 words, this option may not be for you.

The basic elements are:
27 Words / 9 Seconds / 3 Points — including the Ask!

Using the same small hospital foundation as an example, we might come up with something like this:

> Our community has a leading-edge hospital thanks to supporters like you. Protect the future health of your loved ones with a legacy gift to ABC Hospital Foundation.

Is it 27 words? Yes! Can it be said in less than 9 seconds? Yes! Does it have 3 points? We could make the case that there are three:

- Community has a leading-edge hospital,

- It's because of supporters like you, and
- Care will be there for loved ones in future if you make a gift in your Will to the Foundation.

That's a nice tight legacy key message, and one you could easily use for things that require a very bite-sized, concise communication.

But, because of the constraints of the word count, it doesn't have the same emotional feel. It certainly doesn't paint a very vivid picture of the future vision, and since we haven't primed the reader to be thinking long-term, the ask feels a bit abrupt.

However, as I said earlier, one size may not fit all when it comes to key messages.

Maybe you use the first, longer message most widely, but then for brief communications — like your email signature, a prompt in a legacy video, or on social media — you use this short option. You're allowed to adjust as needed and use what works for you in your circumstances.

Do you remember learning the formula
for writing essays in school?
• • •

I used to be annoyed that we had to have an introduction,
three points supporting our position, and a conclusion. Nothing
more, nothing less. It felt overly restrictive, and the best essays
I was reading from authors broke this formula all the time!
15-year-old me longed to be free of what I saw as a stodgy old
formula that no one who wrote for a living ever used.
(Note: I was actually a very agreeable, straight-A student,
who rarely questioned my teachers — lest you think I was
a handful — but it really chafed my chaps!)

I eventually came to see that being able to write to specific
constraints was a useful skill. And I realized that once no one

91

could doubt I knew the rules, I would be free to break them, too. So, the moral of the story is — try these methods, maybe even get good at them — then feel free to take what is useful to you from them and make them your own.

On that note, we have the third option, the Aimée method.

3. Aimée's method for legacy key messages

As the last bit may have foreshadowed, I'm a formula rebel. And yet, here I am, making one of my own.

But I do it for you, dear reader, I swear! After years of seeing how charities struggle to put into words the impact of legacy giving, I sat myself down and said, how can I make this easier for people?

And, while I don't necessarily even follow this formula myself all the time (being a formula rebel and all), I think it is a useful framework.

The basic elements for the Aimée method are:

Donor + Impact + Vision + Ask

Using the same small hospital foundation example, what might this look like?

> You helped realize the dream of building a state of-the-art hospital in [City] *[Donor]* so friends and loved ones can receive the care they need, right here in our community. *[Impact]* And, we're dedicated to continually improving healthcare — for you, and for future generations of [City]ians.

[Vision] As a caring community member you can help — please, consider a gift in your Will to ABC Hospital Foundation. *[Ask]*

We start with the donor. Why? Because years and years of research — in both consumer marketing and fundraising communications — shows that people take notice when they see you are talking about them. So whenever possible, I start with "You", "Your", or the donor's first name if it is a personalized email, letter, or another type of variable messaging piece.

If your legacy message is going to a wider audience, particularly people who aren't necessarily donors at present — you might change the first line to, "Together, we realized the dream of building a state-of-the-art hospital in [City]."

Next, we have the impact. This should be the impact on people and places that mean something to the supporter, for example, their family, their neighbours, their community. It is *not the impact for your organization!* Remember to always highlight the big-picture outward-facing impacts rather than talking about facility upgrades, new equipment, or internal improvements.

The third component is the vision. Legacy gifts are all about the future. So, in our legacy key message we're priming moving forward, like in the mention of "continually improving", and a long time horizon by talking about "future generations".

Lastly, the ask. By the time the reader reaches this point in the message, we've established in their mind that they have the power to make big things a reality (they helped realize the dream of a state-of-the-art hospital), primed their geographic identity, demonstrated the impact for their loved ones and the wider community and got them thinking about the future. Then, right within the ask, we've primed their moral identity as a caring person, and their attachments to others (and sense of social obligation) as a community member. Phew! We did it!

When you break it all down like that it may sound sort of icky or overly calculated, perhaps. The key, for me, is that even though I know the research and am well-versed in all kinds of marketing and psychological priming techniques, the message I create must be authentic. I have to feel it. I have to see and understand why the cause is so important to people.

If you aren't sure why your organization is important enough to people that they would choose to make a legacy gift, take the time to do some investigating before trying to write a legacy key message.

Talk to donors, especially those with long giving histories, even if they don't give large amounts. Talk to program staff, volunteers, and service beneficiaries if possible. Understand deeply why people care, why they give, and why your cause is important in the world. You'll see through their eyes how your organization makes the world a better place, and how your future vision is so compelling and meaningful that people who will never see it come to fruition want to help make it possible for others.

Tips on crafting your legacy message

———

DETERMINE YOUR MESSAGE'S PURPOSE: Start by asking yourself, "What do I want this message to accomplish?" Are you creating awareness? Generating leads? Confirming gifts? Then, ask: "What do I want the reader to think, feel, and do?"

FOCUS ON THE BIG PICTURE: Paint a picture of your organization's big, long-term vision rather than focusing on today's specific needs. This encourages donors to think about the lasting impact of their contributions and helps them see themselves as part of something deeply meaningful.

EMPHASIZE SHARED VALUES AND IMPACT: Highlight the core values your organization and its supporters share, speaking to the donor's moral self. This helps create a connection based on common beliefs and goals. Talk about impact for the cause they care about rather than the importance of having a Will, tax savings, or how other donors found it easy to make these gifts.

SPEAK ABOUT FUTURE GENERATIONS: Focus on the benefits for future generations and use long time horizons in your messaging, ideally looking 50 years or more into the future. This helps donors visualize the enduring significance of their legacy and avoids triggering existential anxiety or death-avoidance behaviours.

USE A HEARTFELT, CONVERSATIONAL TONE: Write in an authentic voice and use conversational language, as if speaking to an individual rather than a crowd. Watch out for slipping into an overly formal organizational voice. And don't forget to try saying it out loud and see if it sounds genuine.

INCLUDE AN ASK! JUST, KEEP IT GENTLE: Encourage people to consider a gift in their Will. Keep the ask soft, making it more of an invitation than a hard appeal. Remember, these are incredibly meaningful decisions for people, and may take 2 to 3 years to act on, so urgency often backfires.

CREATE EMOTIONAL RESONANCE: Aim to create a message that evokes emotions and inspires action. Help people see — and feel — that they can make a lasting difference through their legacy gift.

AVOID NEGATIVE FRAMING: Steer clear of fear or negative framing, such as painting a frightening picture of the future if legacy gifts are not received. Focus on positive outcomes and the beneficial impact of legacy giving. You want people to feel good about their decision.

PERSONALIZE THE MESSAGE: When possible, personalize the message to the reader. Highlight a supporter's long-term connections with your organization and make them feel like a meaningful part of the future work. If you can't personalize, be sure to use the words, "you", and "your", so it feels more like a one-to-one communication.

REMEMBER, IT'S NOT ABOUT YOU: More than any other type of giving, legacy giving is about the person doing it. It's about who they are, what they stand for, and what they want the future to look like. So, make sure your message doesn't solely focus on your organization. Instead, convey a sense of alignment between your vision and the future the donor wishes for. Help donors make the connection that their legacy can help these mutually held values live on through your organization's future work.

Once you have solidified a message that you're happy with, just remember that things can change. Allow your legacy message to be alive. Periodically test it, review it, and revise when needed. That way, you'll ensure it still feels resonant, meets your needs, and is inspiring action among your supporters.

Creating legacy brands, wordmarks, and taglines

Some of the most successful legacy giving programs go one step beyond having a legacy key message and create a legacy brand, wordmark, or tagline.

Creating these elements helps you differentiate your legacy program communications from other messages your donors receive from you. And you anchor the essence of what a legacy gift to your organization means in the minds of donors each and every time they see it.

So, what do we mean when we talk about a legacy brand, wordmark, or tagline?

These words are used virtually interchangeably by many, and while they have some overlap, they're not really the same.

A **BRAND** at its largest scale can mean the holistic identity for your organization — everything that sets you apart in the minds of the public and influences how people perceive and connect with you.

What we're talking about here though is a **VISUAL BRAND**, which refers to the visual elements that contribute to the perception and recognition of your organization. This can be everything from the colours you use, to the fonts, logos, imagery, and any standardized graphic elements that are consistently used across various touchpoints and communication channels.

A visual brand helps people identify and distinguish you from others in your sector and can help differentiate your various programs from each other as well. Your visual brand creates consistency and makes your communications easily recognizable. For instance, you can probably instantly bring to mind the visual image associated with the Red Cross, the United Way logo, and the Canadian Cancer Society's daffodil.

A **WORDMARK** refers to text that has been given a standardized graphic design. These can often be found alongside your organization's logo. Think of The Salvation Army's "Giving Hope Today" wordmark alongside their iconic red shield, or WWF's "For a living planet" beside their initials and panda logo. For our purposes, we'll be talking about a designed version of your legacy program's tagline.

A **TAGLINE** is a short and memorable phrase or slogan used to communicate the essence of your key message. These can be turned into wordmarks, or just be incorporated into your messaging. The examples of "Giving Hope Today" and "For a living planet" would also be considered taglines — it is just the graphic design that makes them wordmarks.

If you're starting from scratch on these three elements, the tagline will be your best place to begin.

Getting started on your legacy tagline

Your legacy tagline is essentially a distilled version of your legacy key message. Ideally in 3 to 8 words or less, it captures the essence of your legacy program, conveying the general idea or feeling that can be absorbed at a glance, without having to read a block of text.

Legacy taglines can have tremendous longevity. In fact, some that I created nearly a decade ago are still in use today, like this one for The Salvation Army of Canada.

This is not uncommon among organizations who opt to create a legacy tagline. Because they are so distilled, they are virtually bedrock, so you will not typically need to update it very often.

Creating a legacy tagline is a real test of your refining skills! How can you sum up what it means to create a legacy for your organization in 3 to 8 words?

The answer is: you go big — *big picture* that is.

Try to answer these questions in just a few words:
  • What is the purpose of your organization? What do you represent in the world?

- What do you do/provide/believe in that no other organization does in the same way?
- Which of your values most resonate with donors?
- When people give to you, what are donors hoping to achieve?
- If your organization could solve one big issue in the world, which one would it be?
- Why does your organization matter to people?
- What is your intended impact on the future?

Keep your responses natural and don't overthink things at this stage. When in doubt, go with your gut.

Some common themes may emerge and that's okay. For instance, you may think of the words *future, hope,* or *improving.*

Your legacy tagline won't necessarily be completely different from every other legacy tagline out there. But, your tagline should be your very best effort to differentiate what makes a legacy gift to your organization special.

This is where your brand personality or voice also comes in. To better understand brand personality, think about Greenpeace. They have a bold, grassroots activist brand personality. Their messaging and even their spray-paint style logo reinforce this. When you think about how they talk to their supporters, it is very different than how a university or hospital foundation communicates with theirs.

You want to keep your organizational voice consistent no matter the topic. Yet sometimes, organizations with very personable brands suddenly adopt a very staid, formal, and prudent tone when it comes to legacy giving. Guard against this tendency so you don't lose your organization's personality when inviting people to consider how powerful their legacy can be. Just be yourself!

Brand personality test:
If your organization were a...

• • •

There's a little exercise I learned many years ago that I like to do if I'm working with an organization on a branding initiative. I have a variety of people at the organization answer some seemingly bizarre questions like:
"If your organization were a vehicle, which vehicle would it be?"

"If your organization were a shoe, what kind of shoe would it be?"

And, "If your organization were a person, what sort of person would it be?"

The answers, and our discussions about them afterwards, are often highly revealing.

These questions require people to think about their organization in ways they never have before, so they get down to very essential impressions of their organization, the work that they do, the impact they have on their community. Because they have no frame of reference for how their organization would like to be seen in these contexts (i.e., what type of vehicle? what type of shoe?), there are no words to fall back on. This can often be an eye-opening exercise.

Do people think your organization is an orthopedic sandal, or a fuzzy slipper, a running shoe, or a shiny black oxford?

If the answers you get aren't how you'd like to be seen, it's often because your messaging is in the wrong voice, or your brand personality isn't well defined.

Putting your
tagline together

Once you've homed in on some key words describing your essence, impact, purpose, why people give to you not similar organizations, and what your values mean to the world, it's time to play with the pieces.

Now, to be honest, putting a tagline together doesn't always happen when I'm sitting at a computer. My mind will mull over the keywords, arranging and rearranging them while I'm washing my hair, or driving, or waiting in a line. So don't fret if you're sitting in front of a blank screen and inspiration doesn't strike right away.

Start by taking all the elements and arranging them in different ways — looking for the order where all the pieces fit best and have the most impact.

Once you have something you're happy with, just as you did with the creation of a key message, let your tagline sit for a day or two, then revisit it and see if there are any extraneous words. See if you can make it shorter. If need be, rearrange the words again. Then, run the tagline by colleagues, family, or friends, to see if they "get it". If they do, great! If they don't, rework further until it is instantly understood — and compelling — to others.

Lastly, I always Google my newly created tagline to ensure it isn't identical something another organization is already using. You don't need to do this with your key message, as they are long enough that it would be pretty difficult to come up with the same wording as another organization. However, because taglines are just a few words, and because some common themes do tend to emerge, I have found that sometimes you can land on the same phrasing.

Personally, I will revise a tagline if I find another organization is already using something I've just created. But some organizations decide they don't mind having the same legacy tagline as another nonprofit as long as the other organization is a step removed in some way — for example, in a different sector or country. Just make sure it genuinely speaks to your organization and your supporters.

I do have a pet peeve about a specific, overused legacy giving tagline format though

• • •

There's one format that has been so overused, that I do actively suggest avoiding it. Not just because it bugs me — and not just because it doesn't really say anything — but because having seen it as much as I have, I know that your supporters have likely seen it many times too. You don't want people to think you're copying other organizations, but whoever's message they've seen first will be the one they think originated it, and every time they see another organization with the same message, they'll think it is phoney.

The format I suggest you avoid? It's the "Your legacy. Their future." style ones. "Your legacy. Their tomorrow." "Their future. Your legacy." "Your legacy. Your impact."

Whatever words you use, and whichever way you rearrange them — it's been overdone. Plus, there's so much more to say about why people make legacy gifts to your organization! So, say something real, something that differentiates, something meaningful.

Creating a legacy wordmark and visual brand

Once you have solidified the words of your tagline, you may decide to have a designer create a visual representation of your message — your legacy wordmark.

The designed wordmark can be created with the intention to appear directly beside your organizational logo on all your legacy material, or simply coordinate with it so that they work well on the same webpage, brochure, or letterhead.

Using a legacy wordmark is a great way to get the repetition count up on the essence of your legacy key message. People will see it and absorb it at a glance, without having to read a block of text. Your legacy wordmark also serves as a visual clue. Every time a supporter sees it, they will know you're talking about legacy giving.

Some organizations like to pair an icon or image with their designed legacy wordmark. This sometimes makes it harder to coordinate with your organization's logo, but you can consider this if it appeals to you. Images chosen often tend to be things like trees, sprouts, winding paths, clasped hands, depictions of older and younger generations, etc. If you decide to go down this route, just make sure you don't veer into overly saccharine imagery or a Freedom 55-type look.

Lastly, you may choose to create a legacy brand, a look that ties all of your legacy messaging together visually. While this can be a trickier one to negotiate with your organization's brand guardians, it can be well worth having the conversation. Legacy donors are not a homogeneous group by any means — but, in general it is still older donors who will be the primary audience for your legacy material.

There are a number of design considerations that are useful to know when creating material for older people, and many of today's organizational brand guidelines do not take these into account. With the majority of graphic designers out there also being decades younger than your average legacy giving audience, there are some things they may not intuitively be aware of. So, while they may favour lightweight sans-serif fonts or reversed text over images, these are often unreadable for older eyes. *And if people can't read your material, they can't be inspired by it!*

This extends to forms and surveys too — handwriting often gets larger as we age, so if you're only leaving a narrow place for people to write their information, those with arthritic hands or poor eyesight are not able to fill it out and return it to you.

To get you started on your legacy brand guidelines, here are my broad recommendations for designing for an older audience:

- Use larger font sizes — ideally 13pt or 14pt for body text.

- Choose serif fonts for body text on your printed material. Serif fonts are more traditional and feel familiar to this particular audience. Plus, for longer blocks of text they improve readability and retention. Sans-serif can be mixed in for headlines and subheads to give variation. This is often the exact opposite of modern brand guidelines — but, making this change not only helps the right people read your legacy material, it also helps differentiate your legacy material from other pieces you may be sending these supporters.

- Whether serif or sans-serif, avoid using overly decorative or thin fonts that can be difficult to discern.

- For your website, sans-serif text is best. It works well at lower resolutions, resizes better and is often the preference of screen readers and digital adaptive technologies — so no need to try to implement a different format for web content.

- Make sure you have good contrast between text and background. Use dark text on a light background for most of your content. If you do any reversed text, it should generally be short in length and on a solid dark background. Avoid low contrast combinations or situations where the contrast varies like text over a photograph.

- Use headings, subheadings, and text formatting (such as bold, underlining, or italics) to segment information and distinguish between different levels of importance.

- Avoid cramming too much content on a page and ensure there is good spacing between lines and paragraphs to make text easier to follow.

- Determine usage guidelines for how your legacy-specific wordmark should be used if you create one. Be sure to include technical specifications like: colour values in CMYK, RGB, and hex colour codes for print and digital use; information on when to use full colour, black, or white versions of the wordmark; details on clear space and margins required around the wordmark; scaling and proportion guidance to ensure consistency across letterhead, envelopes, business cards, and other legacy material; guidelines on how the wordmark should be displayed against different backgrounds (solid colours, gradients, images); and more.

When you have a compelling legacy tagline, a unique wordmark, and a recognizable visual brand, you're giving people something to remember and connect with. Your legacy messaging becomes like a friendly face in a crowd; your supporters can easily spot it and know what to expect.

These elements are not just about crafting an image; they help make your legacy giving message clear, approachable, and memorable. It's about creating an identity that people can connect with and trust, so your legacy giving messaging stands out, and keeps your vision alive in people's hearts until the time is right for them to create a gift in their Will.

ENGAGE AND APPLY

1. Consider the purpose of your legacy key message and the stage you are at with your legacy program — are you trying to build awareness? Generate warm leads? Drive new legacy gift commitments? How would these priorities inform the creation of your legacy message?

2. Which of the three methods of creating a legacy key message feels the most compelling to you and your purposes? Why?

3. How can you tap into the hearts of your supporters through your legacy key message, helping them feel understood and aligned in your shared values?

4. Do any of your organization's other programs have a branded identity or wordmark? Your monthly donor program? Your leadership giving program? How are they used by your organization?

5. How would a legacy brand, wordmark, or tagline help reinforce your legacy message? Where would you see using these components?

THE END.
AND, THE BEGINNING.

_____

We began with my hope that by the end of this book you would feel empowered. Empowered and able to communicate your legacy message simply and easily.

Because it can be simple.

Legacy giving, really, is about what people care about most, and what they want the future to look like. That's all.

When we keep that at the heart of our legacy messaging, people respond.

When you focus on who people are at their core, what they believe in, and their vision of a better world — it feels natural to consider making your organization part of their legacy when you ask.

Help people make these connections within themselves. Help them see how you've been a part of their life story. Help them see how their story can continue with their legacy. Help them dream.

> *"Life begins like a dream,*
> *becomes a little real, and ends like a dream."*
> *— Michael Bassey Johnson,*
> *The Oneironaut's Diary*

I hope this helps you take your next steps with legacy giving — whether you're thinking about it for the first time, sitting down to get started on writing the first legacy messaging for your organization, or looking for new ways to boost your existing legacy program.

Whatever your next step — I hope you take it! And I'd love to hear how it goes for you, so get in touch any time and let me know. Truly!

You can contact Aimée at:
- Email: aimee@refocusfundraising.com
- Find her on LinkedIn — she's the only Aimée Lindenberger there is!

ENDNOTES

1 Miller-Lewis LR, Lewis TW, Tieman J, Rawlings D, Parker D, Sanderson CR. *Words describing feelings about death: A comparison of sentiment for self and others and changes over time.* PLoS One. 2021 Jan 6;16(1):e0242848. doi: 10.1371/journal.pone.0242848. PMID: 33406081; PMCID: PMC7787376.

2 Solomon, S., Greenberg, J., &; Pyszczynski, T. A. (2015). *The Worm at the Core: On the Role of Death in Life.* Random House.

3 James, R. N. (2013). *Inside the Mind of the Bequest Donor: A visual presentation of the neuroscience and psychology of effective planned giving communication* and *James III, R. N., & O'Boyle, M. W. (2014). Charitable estate planning as visualized autobiography: An fMRI study of its neural correlates.* Nonprofit and Voluntary Sector Quarterly, 43(2), 355-373.

4 *Law Times.* (2015, November 2). Many lawyers lack a will despite growing concern. https://www.lawtimesnews.com/news/general/many-lawyers-lack-a-will-despite-growing-concern/261924

5 Iyengar, S. S., & Lepper, M. R. (2006). *When choice is demotivating: Can one desire too much of a good thing? The Construction of Preference,* 300–322. https://doi.org/10.1017/cbo9780511618031.017

6 Alexander Chernev, Ulf Böckenholt, Joseph Goodman, *Choice overload: A conceptual review and meta-analysis,* Journal of Consumer Psychology, Volume 25, Issue 2, 2015, ISSN 1057-7408, https://doi.org/10.1016/j.jcps.2014.08.002. (https://www.sciencedirect.com/science/article/pii/S1057740814000916)

7 Government of Canada, Statistics Canada. (2021, January 26). *Donor rate and average annual donations, by age group.* https://www150.statcan.gc.ca/t1/tbl1/en/tv.action?pid=4510003101

8 Government of Canada, Statistics Canada (2016, April 15). *Volunteering and charitable giving in Canada.* Government of Canada, Statistics Canada. https://www150.statcan.gc.ca/n1/pub/89-652-x/89-652-x2015001-eng.htm#a2

[9] CanadaHelps. (2023, April 10). *The Giving Report 2023.* CanadaHelps. https://www.canadahelps.org/en/the-giving-report/

[10] Fuss, J., Li, N., & Munro, G. (2023, December). *Generosity in Canada: The 2023 generosity index.* fraserinstitute.org. https://www.fraserinstitute.org/sites/default/files/generosity-index-2023.pdf

[11] Canadian Association of Gift Planners. (2020, August 19). *Charitable Giving in Canadian Wills — Current Trends & Opportunities in Legacy Giving.* CAGP Legacy Whitepaper. https://cagp-acpdp.aweb.page/canadiangiftsinwills

[12] Government of Canada, Statistics Canada (2015, November 27). *Reasons for making financial donations, donors aged 15 and over. Chart 8 Reasons for making financial donations, donors aged 15 and over, 2007 and 2010.* https://www150.statcan.gc.ca/n1/pub/11-008-x/2012001/c-g/11637/c-g08-eng.htm

MEET YOUR AUTHOR:
AIMÉE LINDENBERGER,
B.TECH, CFRE

Aimée Lindenberger is well-known in Canada's legacy giving landscape, celebrated for her fundraising communications expertise and innovative approach. With her rich background and diverse lived experience, Aimée brings a unique and inclusive perspective to the field of legacy giving.

Having a powerful combination of education and a wide-ranging career path, Aimée is singularly well-suited to this important work. She holds a degree in Graphic Communications Management, with minors in Marketing and Multimedia, as well as a CFRE designation. In addition, she was privileged to be one of the first in the world to receive a certificate in Philanthropic Psychology, with distinction.

Aimée spent the early days of her professional life in the for-profit sector where she honed her skills in marketing, communications, and project management. Later, inspired by the birth of her children, she shifted focus to make a more meaningful impact, and found her home in the charitable sector.

As the founder of Refocus Fundraising, Aimée specializes in legacy giving and fundraising communications, skillfully blending her expertise with a personal touch to demystify legacy giving marketing for charities. She speaks locally, nationally, and internationally, committed to making these concepts accessible to a wide audience. She has also devoted significant time giving back to the sector, through her volunteer involvement in the Greater Vancouver chapters of the Association of Fundraising Professionals (AFP), the Canadian Association of Gift Planners (CAGP), and as a Knowledge Philanthropist at Vantage Point.

In her ground-breaking book, Aimée Lindenberger doesn't just share knowledge; she opens a door to a new way of thinking about legacy giving. She offers a treasure trove of strategies and insights for charities of all sizes eager to navigate the rewarding world of legacy giving. More than a guide, her book is a beacon, lighting the way for organizations to transform their impact through legacy giving fundraising.

AUTHOR
ACKNOWLEDGMENTS

As I reflect on the process of writing of this book, my heart is full of tremendous gratitude for the people whose support and inspiration have been so important.

First, the dedicated souls in the non-profit sector, and fundraising and legacy giving, in particular. Your tireless efforts to make the world a better place, both now and for future generations, are a constant source of motivation and appreciation. This book is, in many ways, a tribute to all of those doing this important work, and your unrelenting commitment to bettering our world.

I must give a special thank you to my colleague, Jane Westheuser. Her unwavering support and encouragement has been essential throughout the writing process. Jane, your role as my cheerleader, champion, beta reader and more has been indispensable. Without your faith in me and this project, this book may very well have been one of those things on my "I should do that someday" list that I never quite got around to.

To my loving family — *my husband and children* — your support has been essential throughout this endeavour. Thanks for supplying me with endless cups of coffee and your genuine excitement during this busy time. Your patience and love mean the world to me. Thank you.

I am profoundly grateful to my grandparents, whose influence has shaped my path to legacy giving. To my grand-father, the hospital Chaplain who joked with 4-year-old me: "Why do they put fences around graveyards? Because people are *dying* to get in!" and who nearly made 7-year-old me cry thinking about how leaves are at their most beautiful shortly before they fall; you've given me a unique perspective on life's final journey. And to my grandmother, who led teenage me to my first job as a Nurses' Aide in a nursing home. I truly believe that job, caring for people at the end of their life (as she did as well as a Registered Nurse), was the first step towards my career in legacy giving.

Finally, enormous thanks go to the team at Civil Sector Press. Your enthusiasm and belief in this book — and the series — has surpassed my expectations. Your commitment and expertise have been instrumental in bringing this work to the world.

To all of you, my deepest gratitude. This book is not solely a product of my efforts, but a testament to the collective support, wisdom, and kindness that each of you has shared with me.

Aimée
Vancouver, BC
March, 2024

COMING IN 2025
(AND BEYOND!)

The second book in Legacy Giving Essentials — *a ground-breaking, five-part series* — will come out in the spring of 2025!

How to Engage Potential Legacy Donors:
Your Guide to Initial Outreach and Connection

The follow-up to **How to Talk about Legacy Giving** dives deep into the art and strategy of reaching out to potential legacy donors. **How to Engage Potential Legacy Donors** is a comprehensive and essential resource for nonprofit professionals, fundraisers, and charitable organizations seeking effective ways to connect with and inspire individuals to consider legacy giving.

What you'll discover:

- **OUTREACH TECHNIQUES:** Learn how to create surveys, webpages, direct mail campaigns, events, and more that resonate with your audience and encourage them to consider legacy giving.
- **BUILDING CONNECTIONS:** Uncover how to sensitively enquire about legacy interest — and get people to let you know their intentions.
- **REAL-WORLD EXAMPLES:** Draw inspiration from successful legacy giving outreach efforts and apply practical tips to your own outreach strategies.

Pre-order Book 2 now!

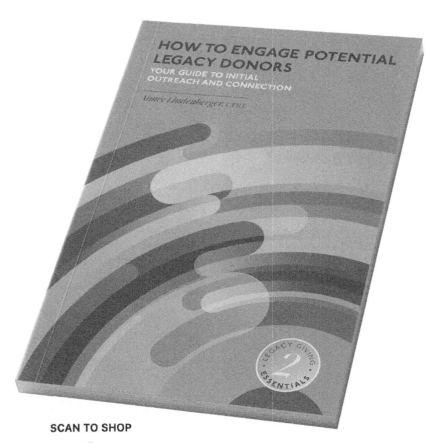

HOW TO ENGAGE POTENTIAL LEGACY DONORS
YOUR GUIDE TO INITIAL
OUTREACH AND CONNECTION

Aimee Lindenberger CFRE

LEGACY GIVING
2
ESSENTIALS

SCAN TO SHOP

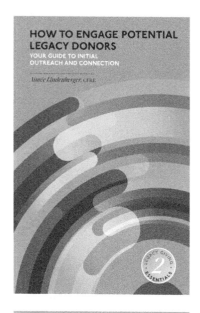

Excited to get your hands on **How to Engage Potential Legacy Donors:** *Your Guide to Initial Outreach and Connection?*

Pre-order your copy today and ensure you're among the first to explore and implement innovative strategies to inspire more people to make meaningful legacy gifts! Take advantage of the pre-order sales price by ordering yours now!

The last three books in this series will be:

How to Cultivate Legacy Gift Commitments:
Your Guide to Moving Interest to Action

How to Steward Legacy Donors:
Your Guide to Deepening Legacy
Donor Relationships

How to Expand the Legacy Conversation:
Your Guide to Engaging Next of Kin,
Honouring Memories, and More

Be the first one to hear when future books are available!

Sign up for Hilborn Charity eNews, a partner business of Civil Sector Press. In free weekly emails, you'll be kept abreast of breaking news on the Canadian nonprofit sector, and read articles offering analysis and tips on fundraising, Boards, leadership, wellness and so much more!

Join our mailing list at **Hilborn-CharityENews.ca**

TESTIMONIALS

Aimée Lindenberger dives deep into the heart — and mind — of the legacy giving decision-making. She transforms research and theory into real-world practice that will make a massive difference for your organization. When you are ready to be inspired, and be inspiring, grab a copy of *How to Talk about Legacy Giving!*

Russell N. James III, J.D., Ph.D., CFP®
Professor & CH Foundation Chair in Personal Financial Planning
Director of Graduate Studies in Charitable Planning
Texas Tech University

Behold, fundraisers! North America's Great Wealth Transfer is underway... and yet will skip most charities. Why? Because nonprofits still don't know how to sell legacy giving all that well! Aimée Lindenberger's speedy new how-to book is your cure.

Tom Ahern
Ahern Donor Communications

Whether you're new to legacy fundraising or a seasoned pro, this book is for you. Aimée guides us through legacy giving science, exploring donors' minds. And she sprinkles in common sense and practical experience while she does it. I've read a lot of legacy-focussed books in my three decades of fundraising. It's now at the top of my list of favourites!

Leah Eustace, MPhil, ACFRE
Executive Director, Advancement,
Faculty of Medicine, University of Ottawa

I am one of many asking Aimée to put fingers to the keyboard and unpack what she has done and taught for over a decade now. Her book is a guided meditation in gift planning, hiding in a rubber-hits-the-road quick read. The secret to unlocking bequests — the biggest untapped capital for Canada's small to medium-sized charities — has been out of reach for many, especially those with one or no full-time fundraising staff, because we make planned giving weird. Aimée translates legalese and successfully de-weirds the building of a sustainable legacy marketing program. This is the plan, the strategy, and most importantly a deep read on the building blocks of what 'legacy' means. Her book can help any organization bring in bequests in a sustainable and approachable way.

Paul Nazareth
VP, Education & Development
Canadian Association of Gift Planners

If you want to understand everything behind legacy giving and how to be comfortable talking about topics that are often difficult to talk about, start here! I absolutely loved this book and would recommend it to anyone working in legacy giving or asking big questions about generosity and end-of-life planning. It takes a lot of care to unpack big and sometimes uncomfortable concepts in such a tangible and engaging way. Aimée has done that beautifully with *How to Talk About Legacy Giving*.

Matt Renzoni
Co-Founder, Willfora

Whether you're an under-resourced fundraiser starting a legacy giving program off the side of your desk or running a well-established program, this book offers practical advice you can incorporate easily and cost-effectively. Aimée's writing has warmth and vitality that's engaging and informative. Her ability to translate complex psychological concepts behind legacy giving into easily digestible insights and practical advice makes this book useful and very accessible. Aimée also shares a wealth of research and wisdom gained from extensive experience in legacy marketing.

This book prompted my own reflection on my involvement in philanthropy as a legacy giving officer and volunteer with CAGP and two charities. It reignited my passion and reminded me of the profound beauty inherent in legacy giving. I found myself immediately applying her insights, quoting stats and snippets to my colleagues. I eagerly await deeper dives into specific subjects in Aimée's future books.

Chantelle Ohrling
Legacy/Planned Giving Officer, Ecojustice
Chair, Communications, CAGP Greater Vancouver

Legacy giving's major challenge is self-inflicted procrastination. It truly doesn't have to be so complicated. This book helps clear the fog and will guide you to a better place. Be prepared to challenge yourself. When you feel it in your heart, you'll know you're on the right path to successful legacy messaging. Let Aimée be your guide.

Daniel Clapin, ACFRE
Retired, Executive Director, Perley Health Foundation
Founding Board Member, CAGP-ACPDP Ottawa Chapter

Made in the USA
Middletown, DE
17 April 2024